C000259018

Short Walks in
Cornwall

Guide to 20 easy walks of 3 hours or less

Published by Collins
An imprint of HarperCollins Publishers
Westerhill Road, Bishopbriggs
Glasgow G64 2QT

www.harpercollins.co.uk

First edition 2011

Copyright © HarperCollins Publishers Ltd 2010

Original text © John H N Mason,
David Perrott and Laurence Main

Collins © is a registered trademark of
HarperCollins Publishers Limited

Mapping on the inner front cover and all
walking planning maps generated from
Collins Bartholomew digital databases

This product uses map data licensed from
Ordnance Survey ® with the permission of the
Controller of Her Majesty's Stationery Office.
© Crown copyright. Licence number 399302

Printed in China by South China Printing Co. Ltd.

ISBN 978 0 00 739545 3

email: roadcheck@harpercollins.co.uk

Contents

Introduction   4
How to use this book   15
Photo credits   96

▶ Short walks

walk 1: Crackington Haven
         4 miles (6.5km)   16

walk 2: Boscastle
         4 miles (6.5km)   20

walk 3: Rough Tor
         2½ miles (4km)   24

walk 4: Cotehele & Calstock
         4 miles (6.5km)   28

walk 5: Polperro to Looe
         5 miles (8km)   32

walk 6: Golant
         3½ miles (5.5km)   36

walk 7: Luxulyan
         3½ miles (5.5km)   40

walk 8: Caerhays &
         Dodman Point
         5 miles (8km)   44

walk 9: Falmouth
         2 miles (3km)   48

walk 10: Lizard Point
         5 miles (8km)   52

walk 11: Gweek
         5 miles (8km)   56

walk 12: Penzance &
         St Michael's Mount
         4 miles (6.5km)   60

walk 13: Merry Maidens
         4 miles (6.5km)   64

walk 14: Sennen Cove &
         Land's End
         4½ miles (7.25km)   68

walk 15: Cape Cornwall &
         Levant
         5 miles (8km)   72

walk 16: Men-an-Tol
         4½ miles (7.25km)   76

walk 17: St Ives
         3 miles (4.75km)   80

walk 18: St Agnes to Porthtowan
         5 miles (8km)   84

walk 19: Porthcothan to
         Mawgan Porth
         4½ miles (7.25km)   88

walk 20: The Rumps &
         Pentire Point
         5 miles (8km)   92

Introduction

Forrabury Stitches

Walking in Cornwall

Cornwall is one of Britain's principal holiday destinations. The county occupies the most southwesterly part of England, a peninsula bounded to the north and west by the Atlantic Ocean and warmed by the waters of the Gulf Stream to an extent that mild winters allow exotic plants to flourish in sheltered places. The sea is never more than 20 miles away and the coast is the main attraction of the county for most visitors. Inland, both the rugged landscape of moorland and the gentler scenery of woodland, valleys and farmland – as well as the remains of over 5000 years of history – are all worthy of exploration. There could be no better way to experience these landscapes than to follow one or more of the routes in this guide. The walks have been carefully chosen to introduce a cross section of countryside, with a selection of places of interest along the way.

Many of the walks include coastal sections and are well signposted for the South West Coast Path. In its entirety this National Trail runs for 630 miles (1014km) around the peninsula from Minehead in Somerset to Poole Harbour in Dorset. To enable the walker to experience selected sections of this path a few of the walks in this guide are planned using public transport to avoid a return journey on foot. In these cases the suggestion is to park your car at the destination and take the bus to the start point of your walk. Always check bus timetables carefully before setting out. Timetables are available locally and online.

Bus: www.westerngreyhound.com covers the Porthcothan to Mawgan Porth walk, the Penzance and St Michael's Mount walk and the Polperro to Looe walk.

www.cornwallpublictransport.info and www.hopleyscoaches.com covers the Hopleys Coaches service between St Agnes and Porthtowan.

Train: as part of the St Ives walk www.firstgreatwestern.co.uk has the timetable for the St Ives Bay Line.

Ferry: it is essential to check ahead for the seasonally operated Tamar Passenger Ferry for the Cotehele and Calstock route. The timetable is available at www.calstockferry.co.uk

A tide timetable gives details of high and low water at various points so you can plan your walks, beach visits and ferry trips accordingly. A visit to Kynance Cove, for example, will be best at low tide when the rock formations are visible, and if you want to walk the causeway to St Michael's Mount then it is essential to visit at low tide. Buy a timetable locally in newsagents or garages, or check out times on the Internet.

Walking is a pastime which can fulfil the needs of everyone. You can adapt it to suit your own preferences and it is one of the healthiest of activities. This guide is for those who just want to walk a few miles. It really doesn't take long to find yourself in some lovely countryside. All the walks are five miles or less so should easily be completed in under three hours. Walking can be anything from an individual pastime to a family stroll, or maybe a group of friends enjoying the fresh air and open spaces of our countryside. There is no need for walking to be competitive and, to get the most from a walk, it shouldn't be regarded simply as a means of covering a given distance in the shortest possible time.

What is Cornwall?

Cornwall is now classified as a county, but it was once a Celtic nation, like Brittany or Wales. This old Celtic Kingdom was where King Arthur and his knights were thought to have roamed, but history and legend have become so entwined that even historians cannot agree. What is certain is that Cornwall has been known for over a thousand years as a place of almost magical attraction.

Cornwall has retained a distinct cultural identity, a legacy from an historic isolation from the rest of the country. The county flag of St Piran, with its white cross on a black background, can be seen flying proudly in many places. The Cornish language was spoken until the 1700s and is still reflected in place names and surnames starting with Tre-, Pol- or Pen-, testifying to an ancient origin. Cornish is now a recognised minority language, which since the early 20th century has benefited from a conscious effort for revival.

Parts of Cornwall are often windswept and treeless, presenting an image of a land of austere grandeur. The wildest place is Bodmin Moor, with its rocky summit tors and boulder-strewn flanks. Cattle, sheep and ponies graze the coarse grasses, bracken and heather. Brown Willy is the county's highest point at 1377ft (420m). Along the coast of north Cornwall the sea has shaped dramatic coastal cliffs and steep-sided valleys. Here the land is gradually eroding under the relentless attack of the Atlantic Ocean. But despite this there are peaceful sheltered coves that are perfect for the holidaymaker, and the scenic beauty is without comparison. In contrast the southern coast provides gentler slopes, green fields and quiet bays of fine sand. The fishing villages are a photographer's delight and everywhere the changeable maritime climate brings the clear light much loved by artists.

Geology

The dramatic and beautiful landscapes of Cornwall are largely a product of the geology beneath. The Lizard peninsula reveals the oldest rocks in the county, with a rare section of serpentine, formed deep in the Earth's crust before being thrust up some 350 million years ago. However, as with the rest of the southwest peninsula, the greater part of the rock structure in Cornwall is of sedimentary origin, formed from beds of mudstone, sandstone and limestone laid down over 300 million years ago on the sea bed or on the beds of lakes. In some places river valleys cut deeply into these sedimentary rocks. In other places immense geological pressures have bent the strata into strange shapes, such as seen in the cliffs along the coast at Crackington Haven.

Rising out of this sedimentary plateau is the granite backbone of Cornwall. Granite is an igneous rock - one that has been thrust up in a molten state into the generally older sedimentary beds, cooling and hardening slowly, sometimes close to the surface. Forces such as the weather and sea have subsequently eroded it, leaving huge exposed bosses, or domes, of which Land's End and Bodmin Moor are examples. The granite of Bodmin Moor was formed 287 million years ago and weathering along lines of weakness in the rock has created the distinctive 'cheesewring' formations often seen on the summits of tors such as Rough Tor. Neolithic Man also made his chamber tombs and entrance graves from the hard granite he found around him and this is one reason why there are more Neolithic remains in the Land's End peninsula than in the whole of the rest of the south-west.

As well as creating the familiar bold and rugged scenery, the formation of granite rocks also made possible the Cornish mining industry. Cooling molten granite had the effect, through immense pressures and heat, of radically changing the sedimentary rock with which it came into contact, forming liquids and gases that eventually solidified as mineral ores. The coastal strip near Land's End, as well as other areas such as St Agnes, are situated on these areas of contact - known as metamorphic aureoles - and this is where the ores of copper, tin and other metals such as silver and gold were found and exploited.

After the mining industry declined another Cornish industry developed that originated from the granite areas of the county. China clay, or kaolin was first discovered in Cornwall in 1746 and is still vitally important to the Cornish economy. Kaolin is granite that has decomposed over millions of years by the action of water originating deep in the earth's crust. The clay is extracted from the quartz by powerful jets of water and the resultant fine-textured, pure white product is used for many purposes, from paper-making to face powder.

North Cornish coast

Wildlife in Cornwall

A diverse landscape produces a diverse flora and fauna, and the walks
in this guide cover a range of habitats from the moorland of Bodmin
and high exposed heath of Land's End to the wooded valleys and warm
sheltered coves of the south coast.

The cliff tops of Cornwall are carpeted in wild flowers. The colours range
from pink thrift to the blue of spring squill and the yellow of golden
samphire. Heather and gorse are plentiful. From the coast paths there
are also some good vantage points to see birds and animals. Grey seals
can sometimes be seen bobbing in the water or sunning themselves on
the shore. The playful bottle-nosed dolphin and the common dolphin
may be spotted from the cliff path, and you may even be lucky enough
to glimpse a pilot whale. Bird life is particularly abundant all along the
coast. On cliff faces you may see herring gulls, great black-backed
and occasionally lesser black-backed gulls, fulmars, kittiwakes and
jackdaws. On other shores you may find shag, cormorant, oyster
catcher, rock pipit, pied wagtail and heron. The rare Cornish chough was
absent for many years but a project is underway to promote the return
of this emblematic bird to the county. Sightings of a wild chough should
always be reported. Cornwall's location on the south-west tip of Britain
means that it also receives many migrant birds. The Island at St Ives,
Land's End and the Lizard are all particularly good for observing the
arrival and departure of migrants, and Marazion Marsh near Penzance is
an important migration stop, particularly for waterfowl and wading birds.

Inland, woodland walks such as Luxulyan will take you through oak, beech,
sycamore and ash. Typical woodland flowers include bluebell and wood
anemone, and there is a wide range of ferns, mosses, lichens and fungi.

Human history

In the warmer conditions after the Ice Age, all Cornwall except the
highest ground became covered by forest. Mesolithic (Mid Stone Age)
Man, who inhabited the land, was probably a nomadic hunter and
fisherman. In about 3500BC Neolithic (New Stone Age) settlers arrived

from the Atlantic seaboard of Europe. They used a variety of stone tools and weapons and founded settlements in forest clearings. Monuments of the Neolithic and Early Bronze Age people are the stone chamber tombs used for communal burials, known as quoits. Surmounted by huge stone slabs and covered originally by earthen mounds, there are a number to be found in Cornwall, including Lanyon Quoit seen on the Men-an-Tol walk. In about 2000BC the Beaker Folk arrived, bringing with them the knowledge of the working of metals. It was they who erected the imposing stone circles and standing stones all over Cornwall. Examples are the Merry Maidens and the Pipers.

The next migrants to reach southern Britain in about 700BC were the Iron Age Celts from northwest Europe. Organised in clans, they were constantly warring among themselves. Characteristic signs of this occupation are hill forts and cliff castles, several of which are passed on walks in this guide. They all feature a steep headland fortified by one or more ramparts, usually built across the narrowest part of the promontory, and The Rumps near Pentire is a good example.

Roman legions landed in Britain in AD43 but do not appear to have bothered much about the small isolated communities in Cornwall, so Roman remains are sparse. After the departure of the Romans in AD410 the Anglo Saxons pushed the Celts into the Welsh mountains and to Cornwall. Many of those reaching Cornwall then crossed to their fellow Celts in France, but others remained, forming a community in Cornwall. The 5th and 6th centuries were remarkable for the number of Welsh, Irish and Breton Christian missionaries who came over to Cornwall, giving many unusual saints' names to churches, towns and villages.

Cornwall had only been a part of Anglo Saxon England for just over 100 years when William the Conqueror landed at Pevensey Bay. By 1072 Cornwall was in Norman hands. The first towns in Cornwall began to spring up and other outward signs of Norman rule began to appear, notably Norman churches.

As with the rest of England, the structure of Cornish life was feudal and the landed gentry built substantial farmhouses. Growing prosperity and settled conditions, coupled with the religious fervour of the Cornish, resulted in a burst of church rebuilding. We owe many of the beautiful 15th century Cornish churches which remain today to this period. The Cornish gentry were wholeheartedly Royalist in the Civil War, and their men followed them into battle. In 1645, however, Cromwell's well-trained forces moved westward and, when Pendennis Castle and St Michael's Mount surrendered after long sieges, the Royalist cause in Cornwall was lost.

With King William III on the throne, Britain seemed to be set for quieter times. Cornwall had a flourishing fishing industry but from 1700 onwards it was mining that developed fastest. Shaft after shaft was sunk to extract ores, and, by the mid 18th century, Cornwall was the largest supplier of copper in the world. The copper boom lasted to about 1870. With new and cheaper sources being discovered abroad, the Cornish mines began to close. The dozens of derelict engine and boiler houses left behind are a familiar feature of the Cornish landscape today and they give an insight into the enormous scale of this industry in what are now relatively remote places. Several of the walks in this guide – St Agnes to Porthtowan, Cotehele and Calstock, Cape Cornwall and Levant, and Luxulyan – fall within areas designated under the Cornwall and West Devon Mining Landscape World Heritage Site.

Cornwall's other traditional industry suffered a severe blow at about the same time as mining. The pilchard shoals, which provided a livelihood for so many fishing villages, disappeared from the coastal waters. There were still mackerel and other fish but there were no longer salted pilchards to send abroad in quantities. Cornish fishing has never fully recovered. In the latter half of the 19th century, the bleak outlook for Cornwall was transformed by the arrival of the railway. Fish, early vegetables and flowers were taken speedily to London and other centres. In the summer, Victorian holidaymakers began to discover the attractions of Cornwall's magnificent coastline and laid the foundations of the present thriving tourist trade.

Walking tips & guidance

Safety

As with all other outdoor activities, walking is safe provided a few simple commonsense rules are followed:

- Make sure you are fit enough to complete the walk;

- Always try to let others know where you intend going, especially if you are walking alone;

- Be clothed adequately for the weather and always wear suitable footwear;

- Always allow plenty of time for the walk, especially if it is longer or harder than you have done before;

- Whatever the distance you plan to walk, always allow plenty of daylight hours unless you are absolutely certain of the route;

- If mist or bad weather come on unexpectedly, do not panic but instead try to remember the last certain feature which you have passed (road, farm, wood, etc.). Then work out your route from that point on the map but be sure of your route before continuing;

- Do not dislodge stones on the high edges: there may be climbers or other walkers on the lower crags and slopes;

- Unfortunately, accidents can happen even on the easiest of walks. If this should be the case and you need the help of others, make sure that the injured person is safe in a place where no further injury is likely to occur. For example, the injured person should not be left on a steep hillside or in danger from falling rocks. If you have a mobile phone and there is a signal, call for assistance. If, however, you are unable to contact help by mobile and you cannot leave anyone with the injured person, and even if they are conscious, try to leave a written note explaining their injuries and whatever you have done in the way of first aid treatment. Make sure you know exactly where you left them and then go to find assistance. Make your way to a telephone, dial 999 and ask for the police or mountain rescue. Unless the accident has happened within easy access of a road, it is the responsibility of the police to arrange evacuation. Always give accurate directions on how to find the casualty and, if possible, give an indication of the injuries involved;

- When walking in open country, learn to keep an eye on the immediate foreground while you admire the scenery or plan the route ahead. This may sound difficult but will enhance your walking experience;

- It's best to walk at a steady pace, always on the flat of the feet as this is less tiring. Try not to walk directly up or downhill. A zigzag route is a more comfortable way of negotiating a slope. Running directly downhill is a major cause of erosion on popular hillsides;

- When walking along a country road, walk on the right, facing the traffic. The exception to this rule is, when approaching a blind bend, the walker should cross over to the left and so have a clear view and also be seen in both directions;

- Finally, always park your car where it will not cause inconvenience to other road users or prevent a farmer from gaining access to his fields. Take any valuables with you or lock them out of sight in the car.

Equipment

Equipment, including clothing, footwear and rucksacks, is essentially a personal thing and depends on several factors, such as the type of activity planned, the time of year, and weather likely to be encountered.

All too often, a novice walker will spend money on a fashionable jacket but will skimp when it comes to buying footwear or a comfortable rucksack. Blistered and tired feet quickly remove all enjoyment from even the most exciting walk and a poorly balanced rucksack will soon feel as though you are carrying a ton of bricks. Well designed equipment is not only more comfortable but, being better made, it is longer lasting.

Clothing should be adequate for the day. In summer, remember to protect your head and neck, which are particularly vulnerable in a strong sun and use sun screen. Wear light woollen socks and lightweight boots or strong shoes. A spare pullover and waterproofs carried in the rucksack should, however, always be there in case you need them.

Winter wear is a much more serious affair. Remember that once the body starts to lose heat, it becomes much less efficient. Jeans are particularly unsuitable for winter wear and can sometimes even be downright dangerous.

Waterproof clothing is an area where it pays to buy the best you can afford. Make sure that the jacket is loose-fitting, windproof and has a generous hood. Waterproof overtrousers will not only offer complete protection in the rain but they are also windproof. Do not be misled by flimsy nylon 'showerproof' items. Remember, too, that garments made from rubberised or plastic material are heavy to carry and wear and they trap body condensation. Your rucksack should have wide, padded carrying straps for comfort.

It is important to wear boots that fit well or shoes with a good moulded sole – blisters can ruin any walk! Woollen socks are much more comfortable than any other fibre. Your clothes should be comfortable and not likely to catch on twigs and bushes.

It is important to carry a compass, preferably one of the 'Silva' type as well as this guide. A smaller scale map covering a wider area can add to the enjoyment of a walk. Binoculars are not essential but are very useful for spotting distant stiles and give added interest to viewpoints and wildlife. Although none of the walks in this guide venture too far from civilisation, on a hot day even the shortest of walks can lead to dehydration so a bottle of water is advisable.

Finally, a small first aid kit is an invaluable help in coping with cuts and other small injuries.

Public Rights of Way

In 1949, the National Parks and Access to the Countryside Act tidied up the law covering rights of way. Following public consultation, maps were drawn up by the Countryside Authorities of England and Wales to show all the rights of way. Copies of these maps are available for public inspection and are invaluable when trying to resolve doubts over little-used footpaths. Once on the map, the right of way is irrefutable.

Right of way means that anyone may walk freely on a defined footpath or ride a horse or pedal cycle along a public bridleway. No one may interfere with this right and the walker is within his rights if he removes any obstruction along the route, provided that he has not set out purposely with the intention of removing that obstruction. All obstructions should be reported to the local Highways Authority.

In England and Wales rights of way fall into three main categories:

- Public Footpaths – for walkers only;

- Bridleways – for passage on foot, horseback, or bicycle;

- Byways – for all the above and for motorized vehicles

Free access to footpaths and bridleways does mean that certain guidelines should be followed as a courtesy to those who live and work in the area. For example, you should only sit down to picnic where it does not interfere with other walkers or the landowner. All gates must be kept closed to prevent stock from straying and dogs must be kept under close control – usually this is interpreted as meaning that they should be kept on a leash. Motor vehicles must not be driven along a public footpath or bridleway without the landowner's consent.

A farmer can put a docile mature beef bull with a herd of cows or heifers, in a field crossed by a public footpath. Beef bulls such as Herefords (usually brown/red colour) are unlikely to be upset by passers by but dairy bulls, like the black and white Friesian, can be dangerous by nature. It is, therefore, illegal for a farmer to let a dairy bull roam loose in a field open to public access.

The Countryside and Rights of Way Act 2000 (the 'right to roam') allows access on foot to areas of legally defined 'open country' – mountain, moor, downland, heath and registered common land. You will find these areas shaded orange on the maps in this guide. It does not allow freedom to walk anywhere. It also increases protection for Sites of Special Scientific Interest, improves wildlife enforcement legislation and allows better management of Areas of Outstanding Natural Beauty.

North Cornish coastal path

The Country Code

The Country Code has been designed not as a set of hard and fast rules, although they do have the backing of the law, but as a statement of commonsense. The code is a gentle reminder of how to behave in the countryside. Walkers should walk with the intention of leaving the place exactly as it was before they arrived. There is a saying that a good walker 'leaves only footprints and takes only photographs', which really sums up the code perfectly.

Never walk more than two abreast on a footpath as you will erode more ground by causing an unnatural widening of paths. Also try to avoid the spread of trodden ground around a boggy area. Mud soon cleans off boots but plant life is slow to grow back once it has been worn away.

Have respect for everything in the countryside, be it those beautiful flowers found along the way or a farmer's gate which is difficult to close.

Stone walls were built at a time when labour costs were a fraction of those today and the special skills required to build or repair them have almost disappeared. Never climb over or onto stone walls; always use stiles and gates.

Dogs which chase sheep can cause them to lose their lambs and a farmer is within his rights if he shoots a dog which he believes is worrying his stock.

The moors and woodlands are often tinder dry in summer, so take care not to start a fire. A fire caused by something as simple as a discarded cigarette can burn for weeks, once it gets deep down into the underlying peat.

When walking across fields or enclosed land, make sure that you read the map carefully and avoid trespassing. As a rule, the line of a footpath or right of way, even when it is not clearly defined on the ground, can usually be followed by lining up stiles or gates.

Obviously flowers and plants encountered on a walk should not be taken but left for others passing to enjoy. To use the excuse 'I have only taken a few' is futile. If everyone only took a few the countryside would be devastated. If young wild animals are encountered they should be left well alone. For instance, if a fawn or a deer calf is discovered lying still in the grass it would be wrong to assume that it has been abandoned. Mothers hide their offspring while they go away to graze and browse and return to them at feeding time. If the animals are touched it could mean that they will be abandoned as the human scent might deter the mother from returning to her offspring. Similarly with baby birds, who have not yet mastered flight; they may appear to have been abandoned but often are being watched by their parents who might be waiting for a walker to pass on before coming out to give flight lesson two!

What appear to be harmful snakes should not be killed because firstly the 'snake' could be a slow worm, which looks like a snake but is really a harmless legless lizard, and second, even if it were an adder (they are quite common) it will escape if given the opportunity. Adders are part of the pattern of nature and should not be persecuted. They rarely bite unless they are handled; a foolish act, which is not uncommon; or trodden on, which is rare, as the snakes are usually basking in full view and are very quick to escape.

Map reading

Some people find map reading so easy that they can open a map and immediately relate it to the area of countryside in which they are standing. To others, a map is as unintelligible as ancient Greek! A map is an accurate but flat picture of the three-dimensional features of the countryside. Features such as roads, streams, woodland and buildings are relatively easy to identify, either from their shape or position. Heights, on the other hand, can be difficult to interpret from the single dimension of a map. The Ordnance Survey 1:25,000 mapping used in this guide shows the contours at 5 metre intervals. Summits and spot heights are also shown.

The best way to estimate the angle of a slope, as shown on any map, is to remember that if the contour lines come close together then the slope is steep – the closer together the contours the steeper the slope.

Learn the symbols for features shown on the map and, when starting out on a walk, line up the map with one or more features, which are recognisable both from the map and on the ground. In this way, the map will be correctly positioned relative to the terrain. It should then only be necessary to look from the map towards the footpath or objective of your walk and then make for it! This process is also useful for determining your position at any time during the walk.

Let's take the skill of map reading one stage further: sometimes there are no easily recognisable features nearby: there may be the odd clump of trees and a building or two but none of them can be related exactly to the map. This is a frequent occurrence but there is a simple answer to the problem and this is where the use of a compass comes in. Simply place the map on the ground, or other flat surface, with the compass held gently above the map. Turn the map until the edge is parallel to the line of the compass needle, which should point to the top of the map. Lay the compass on the map and adjust the position of both, making sure that the compass needle still points to the top of the map and is parallel to the edge. By this method, the map is orientated in a north-south alignment. To find your position on the map, look out for prominent features and draw imaginary lines from them down on to the map. Your position is where these lines cross. This method of map reading takes a little practice before you can become proficient but it is worth the effort.

How to use this book

This book contains route maps and descriptions for 20 walks, with areas of interest indicated by symbols (see below). For each walk particular points of interest are denoted by a number both in the text and on the map (where the number appears in a circle). In the text the route instructions are prefixed by a capital letter. We recommend that you read the whole description, including the fact box at the start of each walk, before setting out.

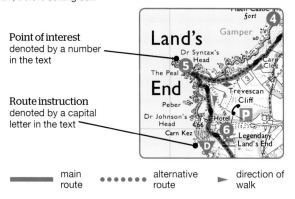

Point of interest
denoted by a number
in the text

Route instruction
denoted by a capital
letter in the text

━━━━ main route
●●●●●●● alternative route
▶ direction of walk

Key to walk symbols
At the start of each walk there is a series of symbols that indicate particular areas of interest associated with the route.

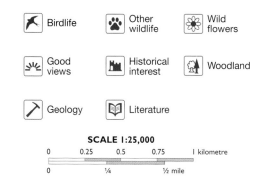

🐦 Birdlife	🐾 Other wildlife	❀ Wild flowers
☀ Good views	🏰 Historical interest	🌲 Woodland
⛏ Geology	📖 Literature	

SCALE 1:25,000

| 0 | 0.25 | 0.5 | 0.75 | 1 kilometre |

| 0 | ¼ | ½ mile |

Please note the scale for walk maps is 1:25,000 unless otherwise stated
North is always at the top of the page

> **The sheer cliffs, rocky reefs and wide open views seen from this route are typical of the dramatic scenery of the north Cornish coast**

The folded and contorted rocks in the cliff-faces of this coastline have become known as the 'Crackington Formation'. 80 million years of sedimentation has been compacted and overturned to create the features we see today. The distinctive geology makes for an interesting route, with an undulating path and a steep-sided coombe to cross. When walking the high cliff top path you are aware of the force of the Atlantic waves below you and it is easy to see why so many ships have been wrecked on the rocks of this coast.

Although Crackington is best-known for its geological importance there is also much historical interest along this route. Peaceful St Gennys church and its poignant gravestones are reminders of the communities that once lived here.

Crackington Haven

View over Crackington Haven

Route instructions

1 The huge 430ft (130m) cliffs, with their strangely contorted rock strata, tower above the small collection of houses, café, shop and 300 year old Coombe Barton Inn. Crackington Haven was once a small port for importing coal and limestone from Wales, and exporting slate from local quarries. The lime-rich beach sand was in such demand that by the 1800s the beach was excavated down to its bedrock. It is now sandy again, and very popular with surfers.

A Park in the large Crackington Haven car park and take the narrow path from the far end of the car park. Turn right onto the road and follow it uphill.

2 These old thatched cottages, now called 'Old Cottage' and 'Pa's Cottage' are possibly of medieval origin and were originally one longhouse typical of a Cornish yeoman farmer at the time, when one building housed both family and livestock under one roof. They are now holiday cottages.

B At the crossroads turn left past the entrance of the house 'Nancemellan'. At the lane junction turn left.

3 The church of St Gennys, with its steeply sloping chuchyard, lies in an idyllic situation at the end of the lane and is worth a visit. Parts of the tower and chancel are

Plan your walk

DISTANCE: 4 miles (6.5km)

TIME: 3 hours

START/END: SX143968 Park in the large car park near Crackington Haven beach, or there is another car park further up the hill past the Coombe Barton Inn.

TERRAIN: Strenuous; some steep slopes

MAPS:
OS Explorer 111;
OS Landranger 190

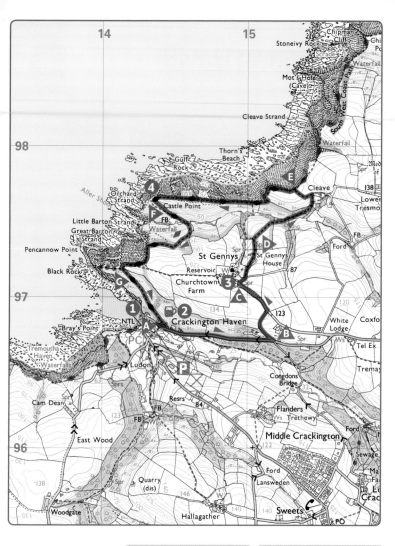

Norman although much of the building dates from the 15th century. The graveyard contains many graves of shipwrecked mariners. On the right hand side of the church path, tucked into the slope of the green, is the stone-roofed St Gennys well, thought to date from the 6th century.

▷ At the next junction turn left again to explore the church before returning to go straight ahead, following

Crackington Haven

the lane downhill with 'Old School House' on your left. Go through the gate of St Gennys House, signposted as a footpath, and follow the driveway down. Continue on the track to the right of the house then go over a stile.

D Follow the field boundary with the hedge on your left then cut across the field to your right, descending to the woodland below. Follow the path through the woodland to emerge at a stile. Follow two sides of the field with the boundary on your right before turning left on the cliff top to join the coast path.

E Follow the well-defined coast path to Castle Point.

4 This cliff top castle site dates from between 350BC and 150BC and was the most northerly of Cornwall's cliff castles.

F Follow the zig-zag path to descend and ascend a steep-sided coombe to bring you above Pencannow Point.

G After rounding the headland a track runs diagonally straight down the hillside to emerge on the road next to the longhouse cottages. Turn left to return to the car park.

View north from Pencannow Point

66 A lovely varied walk exploring the coast and countryside around the historic village of Boscastle and the beautiful wooded valley of the Valency **99**

From the harbour this route climbs up the coast path for fine views from Willapark before turning inland past the ancient strip system of cultivation on Forrabury Common. It continues through the village of Boscastle, across farmland and along woodland paths to follow the course of the peaceful Valency River down the valley back to the start. Along the way there are reminders that this was a village devastated by a sudden flash flood on 16th August 2004. The car park at the start of this walk had a 10ft (3m) wall of water raging through it at 40mph that afternoon. Since then the community has worked together on a programme of rebuilding and regeneration, and this walk is testimony that Boscastle once again has much to offer visitors.

Stepping stones, Valency River

Boscastle

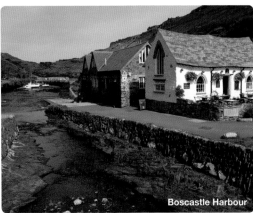

Boscastle Harbour

Route instructions

A Park at Boscastle car park. Leave by the main entrance and follow the road through the village to the riverside track. Cross the bridge and continue to the quayside, with the river now on your right.

1 The harbour was built in the late 16th century. From then until the end of the 19th century Boscastle was mainly a fishing village, pressing and preserving pilchards near the harbour. As an important port in the 19th century, Boscastle imported coal and lime from Wales and exported ores from local mines. In the aftermath of the 2004 flood, 84 wrecked cars were found in the harbour, with many others washed out to sea.

Although incredibly no lives were lost, 58 properties were flooded, four of which were demolished, including the Visitor Centre, which has since been rebuilt. The limekiln next to the Visitor Centre dates from the late 1700s and is one of two that were originally in Boscastle.

B Go up the steps next to the breakwater and turn left onto the coast path. Note the view of Meachard, an island rock with seabird colonies. Continue straight on and ignore the path to the left signposted 'Circular Walk'. At the path junction bear right, signposted 'Willapark'. Follow the path to the Coastwatch Lookout.

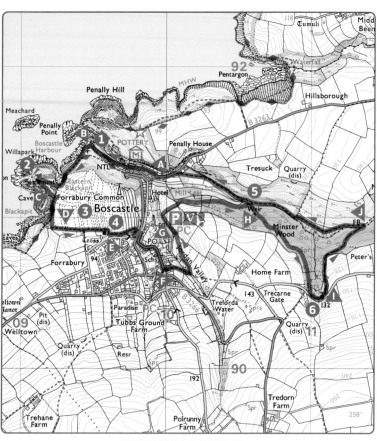

2 The volcanic headland of Willapark, meaning 'look out' was the site of an Iron Age promontory fort. The white-painted Lookout on the summit is manned by National Coastwatch Institute volunteers, but was originally built in 1827 as a 'pleasure house' by the merchant Thomas Avery. On clear days there are views north as far as Hartland Point and Lundy Island.

C Bear right as you descend

the headland. Go through a gate and turn right to rejoin the coast path.

D Bear left at the next fork to follow the path around Forrabury Stitches to the churchyard.

3 Forrabury Stitches is one of the few examples left of a medieval system whereby strips of land are cultivated on a four-year rotation. The strips are clearly visible from the path.

Boscastle

4 St Symphorian's church was mostly rebuilt in 1867, although the original building was 12th century. Outside the churchyard is Forrabury Cross, a medieval cross once used as a gatepost.

E Go through the churchyard, turn left, go through a gate, then turn left to follow a field edge. Go through a stile on your right. Cross the main road. Go down the side road opposite and turn right at the junction to continue up the road.

F Turn left onto the path near the top of the street, just before the main road. Go between the house and a small pond to walk with a stream on your right. Pass the wooden bridge and go through the kissing gate. Turn left onto the path marked 'Home Farm' and signposted 'Minster Wood'. Following the hedge on your left, cross two fields over two stiles. Cross the next field and go through a gap in the opposite hedge to the gate in the corner of the field to enter Cold Frame Orchard.

G Exit the orchard over the stile and keep left along hedge boundaries. Cross another stile then follow the faint track diagonally across the field to a gate. Follow the track signposted 'Valency Valley' through Minster Wood.

5 With the river crossable by stepping stones, it can be hard to imagine the Valency River in full torrent. The valley landscape changed considerably after the 2004 floods, but the riverside meadows and woodland soon showed signs of recovery and became rich in wildlife again. For a shorter route back to the car park cross the stepping stones here and turn left to follow the valley path.

H With the river on your left climb to follow the woodland path to Minster Church. Emerge on a lane, turn left then left again through the church gate.

6 This church, nestled in its secluded woodland setting, is the mother church of Boscastle. The site has been a place of worship since 500AD and within the churchyard, at the bottom of the slope, is the Holy Well of St Madrun.

I Go down the steps below the church and through a kissing gate to follow the path through St Peters Wood.

J Cross the Valency River over the wooden footbridge. Turn left and follow the path back to the car park.

Forrabury Church

> **❝** Rough Tor is a fine example of Bodmin Moor's granite landscape and this walk reveals breathtaking scenery after a surprisingly short, though steep, ascent **❞**

This is a very pleasant walk on a fine day, when panoramic views reward you for a fairly strenuous climb. On a clear day it is possible to see both the north and south coasts of Cornwall from the summit. In low visibility this walk should not be attempted at all.

Bodmin Moor is the wildest place in Cornwall and Rough Tor is its second highest spot at 1311ft (400m). The ridge is impressively rough, being littered with huge slabs of granite which have been dramatically weathered. There is peace, solitude and the sound of skylarks.

View from the summit, Rough Tor

Rough Tor

Logan-stone

Route instructions

A Start from the Forestry Commission car park. This is below Rough Tor at the end of a lane, Roughtor Road, which leaves the A39 on the northern edge of Camelford and leads over 2 miles (3.2km) south eastwards to the high moorland.

With the tors ahead, go ahead through a gate at the bottom of the car park.

B Cross a slab bridge over a stream and go ahead up a wide grassy path. Veer left towards Showery Tor, a rocky outcrop on your far left. This is surmounted by a 'cheesewring', a rock feature. Turn right along the ridge to Rough Tor, with its magnificent views.

1 At the summit of Showery Tor is a spectacular 16ft (5m) 'cheesewring' formation, sitting central in a 98ft (30m) wide Bronze Age cairn circle.

2 Across the moorland to the south-east Brown Willy can be seen, the highest spot in Cornwall at 1375ft (420m). Rough Tor isn't much lower at 1311ft (400m). In the opposite direction the vast china clay pit and settling lake of the former Stannon Works is visible. It was the last of Bodmin Moor's clay works, closing in 2003. When it was in production powerful streams of water separated the china clay in decomposed granite from the accompanying quartz and

DISTANCE: 2½ miles (4km)

TIME: 1½ hours

START/END: SX139819

TERRAIN: Strenuous

MAPS:
OS Explorer 109;
OS Landranger 200

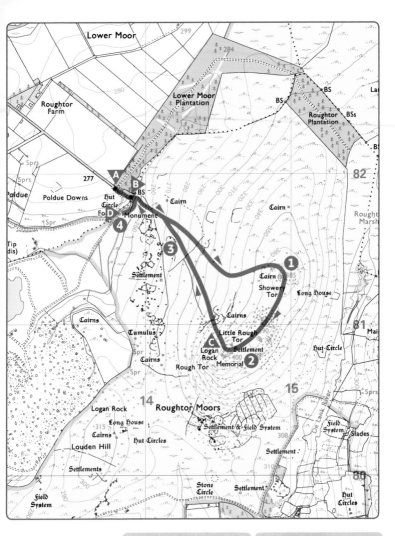

mica. The result was a pure white mud, which was dried in long, heated sheds. The china clay was exported and the waste quartz was left in large heaps.

A medieval chapel dedicated to St Michael once marked Rough Tor's summit, which now bears a plaque in memory of the 43rd (Wessex) Division, who trained here. Their sacrifices during World War II prompted Sir Richard Onslow, the former landowner, to present this

Rough Tor

land to the National Trust in 1951, in their memory. The plaque faces a logan-stone, a rock poised to sway at a touch. A basin may have been scooped out of its top to contain a beacon fire or sacrificial blood. In areas of china clay extraction look out for the blue of amethyst quartz in moorland streams.

3 Look out for Bronze Age (1800BC) oval enclosures and hut circles here. The enclosures were paddocks made with stones cleared from the fields.

C Descend directly down towards the car park, initially picking your way through the granite boulders of the slope, then following the path straight ahead. Just before the bridge, turn left over the stile to see the monument.

D Retrace your steps to the bridge, go left across it and climb back up to the car park.

4 The monument is a granite column erected by public subscription in memory of a young servant-girl, Charlotte Dymonde, who was murdered here on Sunday, 14 April 1844, by a fellow servant, Matthew Weekes.

Charlotte Dymonde monument

66 This route explores a section of the River Tamar and passes through the historic village of Calstock, providing varied walking through woodlands and along the river bank 99

Part of the route follows the way-marked Tamar Valley Discovery Trail and the walk will give you a feel for the historical importance of the River Tamar. Plan your walk carefully and you will be able to return on the Tamar Passenger Ferry, getting a perspective of the Tamar from the river itself whilst enjoying views of the steep wooded banks at a leisurely pace. Ferry operating days vary according to the tide, and the service is only available in summer, so it is essential to check timetables in advance. Part of the walk is also within the Cotehele estate and if there is time it is worthwhile to combine your walk with a visit to Cotehele House, one of the finest Tudor manor houses in England.

Cotehele & Calstock

Cotehele House

Route instructions

1 Cotehele Quay was a thriving port in the 19th century. The 18th and 19th century buildings that remain include a block of half-arch limekilns, typical of others in the area. Moored on the quayside is the *Shamrock*, a restored Tamar sailing barge built in 1899. Ketch-rigged and 57ft (17m) long, she represents a type of boat unique to the River Tamar and surrounding waterways. The Discovery Centre houses displays on the Tamar, boat building, the lime trade and the *Shamrock*.

A Take the path running alongside the car park and walk northwards away from the quay. Bear right at the junction to follow the path through the woods.

2 The simple, single-cell Chapel in the Woods was built in the late 15th century by Sir Richard Edgcumbe, the builder of Cotehele House, to give thanks for his escape from Richard III in these woods in 1483.

B Pass the chapel on your right and continue along the wide path with the river below you. As the path steepens and bends to the left there is a viewpoint – the Calstock Lookout – with a splendid view of the meandering river and village of Calstock. Continue upwards through the woodland, turning right at the path junction to follow the signpost to Calstock, then descending towards the Danescoombe valley.

Plan your walk

DISTANCE: 4 miles (6.5km)

TIME: 2½ hours plus either allow time for ferry (¼ hour journey) or an additional ¾ hour to walk back

START/END: SX423681 Cotehele Quay

TERRAIN: Easy

MAPS:
OS Explorer 108;
OS Landranger 201

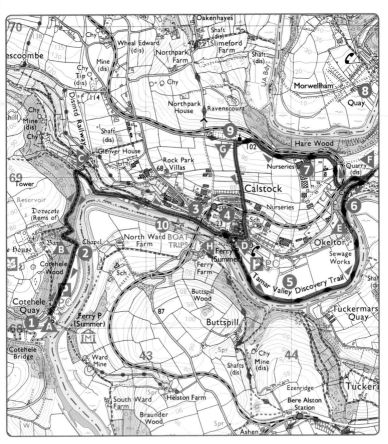

At the junction with a track turn right past cottages on your left. Continue along the metalled road passing two sets of limekilns on your left and boatyards and a chandlery on your right. Walk under the viaduct.

3 This magnificent 120ft (37m) high viaduct was built between 1904 and 1907. Constructed from over 11,000 reinforced concrete blocks the overall look nevertheless appears to be

of stone. It now carries the scenic Tamar Valley branch line which runs between Plymouth and Gunnislake.

4 Calstock was once a flourishing port, shipping out copper, tin, arsenic and granite. The return trade in coal, limestone and 'dock-dung' supplied the mining industry, lime-kilns and market gardens of the area.

At the road junction turn right, then right again down

Cotehele & Calstock

to the quay. If you plan to return by ferry now is the time to check ferry times on the board by the jetty. Then facing the river turn left to follow the riverside path. Pass playing fields on your left and go through the gate for the Tamar Valley Discovery Trail, following the raised path alongside the bank of the river.

5 The reed beds of the Tamar are important wildlife habitats, especially for bird and insect species.

E▶ Go through the kissing gate and head straight ahead, uphill through the gate for the Okeltor Wildlife Reserve, following the wooded track.

6 By following the path on your right it is possible to detour to see the former mine workings of Okeltor more closely.

F▶ Pass the chimney on your right. Go through the gate and turn left onto the metalled lane. At the road junction turn right and proceed with care over the level crossing. Follow the lane uphill as it bends to the left. Continue along the lane until you reach the church on your right.

7 Along this section of the route there are entrances to nurseries. The Tamar valley

was once an important centre of market gardening and fruit-growing, supplying the markets of Covent Garden in London and other cities. The sheltered hillsides are still used for this purpose, although on a much smaller scale since World War II.

8 There are glimpses through the trees to another section of the Tamar as it meanders past Morwellham Quay in Devon.

9 15th century St Andrews Church is unusual for having a stone fireplace in its porch.

G▶ Turn left at the road junction in front of the church and follow the lane down into Calstock village. Turn right at the bottom of Church Street and follow the road, bearing left, down to the quay.

10 During the summer the traditional open wooden boat of the Tamar Passenger Ferry operates between Calstock, Cotehele and Ferry Farm in Devon. There are also trips up river from Calstock to experience a particularly tranquil section of the river.

H▶ Either take the ferry to return to Cotehele Quay by river, or retrace your steps back along the riverside road and through the woods to the car park.

St Andrews Church

“ Walk the coast path between two of Cornwall's most well-known and historic fishing villages and experience the solitude of the path between them ”

To avoid retracing your steps for the return journey, use the regular 573 bus service between Looe and Polperro. Park in one of the several car parks in Looe and take the bus to Polperro, walking back to Looe on a well-defined path along a scenic stretch of coastline. Both Looe and Polperro can be very busy places in summer so this walk gives the opportunity to see thriving tourism as well as enjoying the more peaceful coastline in between. From the path dolphins can sometimes be seen offshore.

Polperro to Looe

Crumplehorn Inn

Route instructions

A Park in one of the Looe carparks, although be aware that the car parks can fill quickly in summer. Catch a bus to Polperro from the bus stop across the road from the bridge in East Looe.

1 Until 1832 West and East Looe were two separate communities. Both communities were granted charters in the 13th century and were important fishing ports with smuggling as a sideline. There is a sandy beach at East Looe, two medieval churches, a museum and a wide selection of shops and restaurants. A small passenger ferry crosses between East and West Looe, and there are boat trips up the river.

B From the bus stop at Crumplehorn walk downhill with the Crumplehorn Inn on your left. Follow the road down to Polperro harbour.

2 The 16th century Crumplehorn Inn and Mill has a working water wheel. Parking for Polperro is at Crumplehorn because vehicular access to the village is strictly controlled.

3 Despite its popularity this former fishing village and centre of smuggling has kept something of the atmosphere of a Cornish fishing village, with colour-washed cottages, winding streets and a small harbour. At the harbour is the Polperro Museum of Smuggling and Fishing.

Plan your walk

Bideford
Bude
Launceston
Wadebridge · Bodmin
Newquay · Liskeard
St Ives · Truro · St Austell
Falmouth
Penzance
Land's End

DISTANCE: 5 miles (8km)

TIME: 3 hours

START/END: SX255535 One of several car parks in Looe

TERRAIN: Moderate

MAPS:
OS Explorer 107;
OS Landranger 201

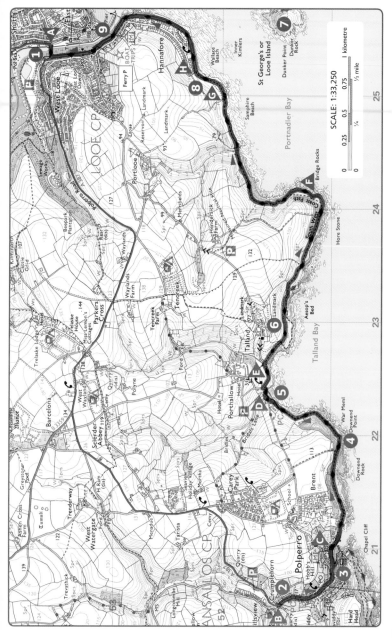

Polperro to Looe

C Follow the narrow street uphill from the east end of the harbour which brings you out on to the coast path, signposted for Talland Bay. From here the route follows the well marked cliffpath round the headland of Downend Point.

4 The cross on your right is a memorial to the people of Talland and Polperro who died in World Wars I and II.

D The coastal path route around the western side of Talland Bay is only possible on the seaward side at low tide. The path joins a narrow lane just before Talland, then on a left hand bend becomes a path again as it drops down to Talland Bay.

5 Talland Bay has a small sandy beach and a seasonally open café.

E Take the road up out of Talland Bay, turning right at the junction. Follow the road until the path to Looe on the right, opposite the café. From here the path follows the coastline on the fringe of the West Looe Down, which is pleasant open pastureland sloping 300ft (91m) down to the sea.

6 Shortly after leaving Talland you will see two high landmarks which denote one end of a nautical mile for naval speed trials.

F Continue along the coast path, rounding Portnadler Bay, with views out to Looe Island.

7 Looe Island, ½ mile (750m) off Hannafore Point, is also called St George's Island and more historically, Lamanna. It was once a thriving religious community but is now a natural sanctuary for birds. Boat trips from Looe make the island accessible to day visitors in summer.

G On the downs before you reach Looe there is a signposted path on the hillside to your left to the foundations of the ancient chapel of Lammanna.

8 Only a few low wall sections of this ancient Celtic chapel remain. The site is believed to be a partner site for the 11th century Lammanna chapel on Looe Island.

H The path enters Looe at Marine Drive, a promenade with large houses on the landward side. Continue along the seafront road to the centre of Looe.

9 On your way along the waters edge you pass Nelson, a bronze sculpture of a grey seal who was a familiar sight in south Cornish harbours for over 25 years.

❝ From the tidal harbour of Golant, this peaceful walk follows the river south then turns inland along wooded paths and tracks through quiet countryside **❞**

The River Fowey is at its most beautiful when passing Golant, and this walk initially follows a path parallel to the river, with its wooded slopes and moored yachts. Sheltered lanes are taken inland until again the river valley comes into view by St Sampson's Church. Part of this route follows The Saint's Way (*Forth an Syns* in Cornish), a path crossing Cornwall from Padstow in the north to Fowey in the south.

Golant

St Sampson's Church

Plan your walk

Bideford
Bude
Launceston
Wadebridge Bodmin
Newquay Liskeard
St Ives Truro St Austell
Falmouth
Penzance
Land's End

DISTANCE: 3½ miles (5.5km)

TIME: 2½ hours

START/END: SX120552

TERRAIN: Easy; muddy in places

MAPS:
OS Explorer 107;
OS Landranger 200

Route instructions

A From Lostwithiel take the A390 to St Austell. After about 1½ miles (2.4km), turn left on the B3269 towards Fowey. Then, after 3 miles (4.8km), turn left at Castledore, following the sign for Golant. Take the left turn at the next junction, signposted to the church not to Golant. When St Sampson's Church appears on a bend, you will see a wide layby on the right. Park here.

From the church, walk down the hill towards Golant. Turn left at the crossroads by a former chapel, and walk down to the tidal harbour. Walk alongside the harbour and turn right by the Fisherman's Arms.

1 Golant was known as Golenanta in the 15th century, and means 'the fair in the valley'. It is a picturesque village of small cottages around the Fisherman's Arms pub, and rises steeply behind a tidal anchorage enclosed by a railway line. This line, which carried passenger trains to Golant Station until the 1960s, is still in use, but only for the transport of china clay to the docks above Fowey. The old quay, which once served trading craft, is now surrounded only by yachts and dinghys.

B Turn left at the T-junction. When the road ends continue straight ahead along the path.

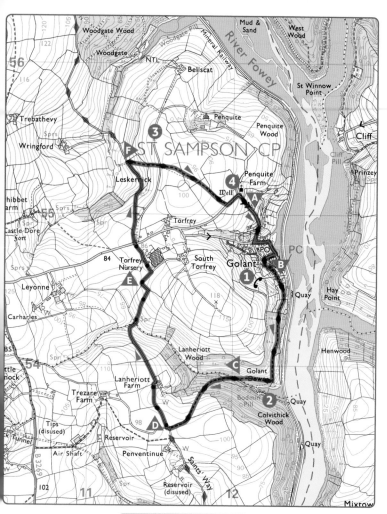

2 Bodmin Pill was used as a tidal harbour by the merchants of Bodmin in medieval times, who wished to avoid paying harbour dues at Fowey. Pill is a Celtic word signifying a tidal creek.

▶ The path descends around Bodmin Pill and crosses a wooden bridge over a small stream. Turn right immediately after the stream, and walk uphill along a track through trees. When the path forks, go to the right, uphill. As you leave the trees, go through a stile and follow the path to the left of a hedgerow ahead.

Golant

Continue with the hedgerow on your right. Go through a stile to join a road by some sheds.

D Turn right following the lane, bearing left onto a track next to Lanheriot Farm. Cross a stile and continue following the path uphill. Turn left as the path becomes a grassy track.

E When the track joins a tarmac surfaced lane, turn left to reach a crossroads. Go ahead along a lane to the left of the entrance to the Youth Hostel driveway.

F After about 600yds (550m), turn right at a stile indicated by a Saint's Way waymark. Walk across the field to a stile on the far right hand side. Cross it. Walk with a hedge on your left to cross another stile. Cross the lane and another stile, then walk across a large field to a waymarked crossing point over the fence. Walk ahead to join a hedge on your left. Follow the hedge to reach a stile onto the lane opposite the parking layby.

3 This road is the driveway to Golant Youth Hostel at Penquite House, a fine Italianate stucco mansion built circa 1840 by Colonel Peard. One of his friends was the Italian politician Garibaldi, who stayed here in 1864.

4 St Sampson's Church stands in a superb elevated position overlooking the River Fowey, built beside a holy well which is now enclosed to the left of the porch. Its founder, Sampson, who was born in Glamorgan in the 6th century, was the son of Amwn Ddu of Mawddwy and Anna of Gwent, King Arthur's sister. Apprenticed at Illtyd (now Llantwit Major), Sampson began his missionary work in Cornwall, where he found a pagan tribe led by Gwedian. He converted them to Christianity, it is said, by bringing back to life a boy killed in a riding accident. Gwedian and his tribe, now convinced of Sampson's holy power, asked him to rid them of a troublesome serpent, which lived in a cave just ½ mile (0.8km) from Golant. After wading across the river, Sampson entered the serpent's dark lair and, invoking the name of Jesus Christ, killed the beast. He then instructed his followers to build a monastery, and continued his travels to Brittany. The present church, consecrated in 1509, is considered to occupy this site. The Trystan Stone, which now stands at 'Four Turnings', on the A3082, 1 mile (1.6km) to the north-west of Fowey, was taken from St Sampson's.

Bodmin Pill

> **66** A peaceful walk exploring an extraordinary concentration of industrial heritage within a valley long recognized as being of great natural beauty **99**

This fine walk along the narrow wooded valley of Luxulyan is packed with interest. Despite being part of the Cornish Mining World Heritage Site, the valley is quiet, with an unearthly atmosphere all of its own. In the 19th century the valley was used as a transport route for local mines and quarries. In the early 20th century it became important for the processing of china clay. Many of the paths on this route are alongside watercourses, and industrial archaeology abounds. Nature lovers will also appreciate the wide variety of plant and animal life in the woodland and freshwater habitats.

Luxulyan

Bridge over the Carmears Incline

Route instructions

1 The church of Saints Cyriacus and Julitta is a fine 15th century building constructed from local granite. The village of Luxulyan grew up around the church and was once a hive of activity based on mining and quarrying.

A Park on the road opposite the church. With the church on your left walk down the hill to the well on your left.

2 This holy well, now dry, is dedicated to St Cyor, an early Celtic saint. The restored wellhouse was built in 1412.

B Continue on the road out of the village. After crossing a small bridge over a stream, turn right along a lane signposted 'Luxulyan Valley'.

C When a lane joins from the left, go ahead between granite posts. Walk through the car park then bear left through trees for about 50yds (45m) to climb the steps to a small embankment containing a leat (watercourse). Walk with the leat on your left, passing under the viaduct and continuing for about ¾ mile (1.2km).

3 Carmears Wheelpit is the site of a mid 19th century waterwheel, 30ft (9m) in diameter, built to wind wagons up the incline. Wagons were connected to the waterwheel by a wire rope. In the late 19th century a larger replacement wheel at the site powered china clay mills.

Plan your walk

DISTANCE: 3½ miles (5.5km)

TIME: 2 hours

START/END: SX052580 Roadside parking opposite the church in Luxulyan village

TERRAIN: Moderate; but can be muddy

MAPS:
OS Explorer 107;
OS Landranger 200

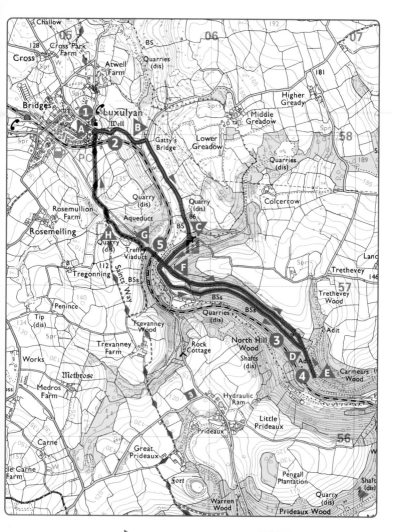

D About 130yds (120m) beyond the wheelpit, the track of the old incline passes obliquely over the leat. Walk downhill as far as the stone bridge over the incline.

of the Carmears incline, opened in 1841, where trucks carrying crushed minerals from Ponts Mill were pulled up the 1 in 10 slope by wire rope.

4 Granite sleepers lie embedded in the ground

E Retrace your steps, following the incline uphill

Luxulyan

and bearing right to walk above the waterwheel. Follow the path alongside another leat parallel to, but above, your outward path.

▶ As the leat goes underground the Treffry Viaduct appears straight ahead. Continue ahead, walking across the viaduct.

⑤ Planned by Joseph Thomas Treffry, this impressive granite viaduct was built between 1839 and 1842 to carry a horse drawn tramway.

▶ At the end of the viaduct go up the wooden steps on your left to enter a field. Turn right at the wooden post and cross the stile ahead of you. Follow the path, turning right at a junction to cross two small footbridges, and go over a stile.

▶ Walk along a distinct green track, following the wooden marker posts to some stone steps over a wall on your left. Climb over and walk along the right hand edge of a field. Go through a gateway, cross a track and enter a second field. Go through another gateway ahead and follow the obvious pathway across two fields back to the church.

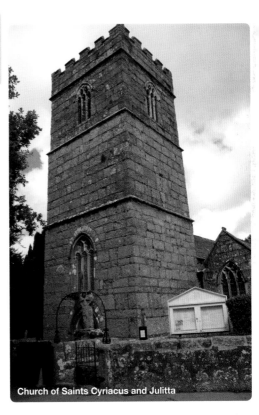

Church of Saints Cyriacus and Julitta

> 66 From the scenic setting of Caerhays there is a climb to one of the highest points on the south Cornish coast, rewarded on a fine day with views to as far west as the Lizard and east to Rame Head near Plymouth 99

The starting point of the walk is at Porthluney Cove, a popular wide sandy beach with a large parking area. There is easy access to the beach from the car park and the refreshment booth is open from Easter to September. The beach, which provides good, safe swimming, is in a beautiful setting of wood, stream and pasture with Caerhays Castle as a centrepiece. From here the walk follows a dramatic section of coastal path before the turning point at Dodman, the most prominent headland between Falmouth and Plymouth. Although the return route involves a road section, it is pleasant walking through some typical Cornish countryside, and the relatively level route may well be welcome after the ascents and descents of the earlier coastal path. As you return to Porthluney a stunning view of Caerhays Castle and the valley opens up before you.

Approaching Hemmick Beach

Caerhays & Dodman Point

Caerhays Castle

Route instructions

1 Caerhays Castle was built in 1808 by John Nash on the site of a much older manor house. The castle grounds have been used many times as a film location over the years, most famously as the setting for Manderley in the 1979 TV production of Daphne du Maurier's novel *Rebecca*. The gardens are home to the National Magnolia Collection, and are also known for their displays of camellias and rhododendrons. Both castle and gardens have restricted opening times.

A Park in the beach car park at Porthluney Cove. Leave the car park at the entrance gate and turn right onto the road. Go through the kissing gate on the roadside opposite the castle gatehouse, signposted to Hemmick. Follow the track running up across a field. Go over a stile and keep to the seaward boundary of the next field to go through another kissing gate. Climb steadily through a copse and emerge above the bay bounded on the east by Greeb Point, with fine views ahead of you.

B Follow the well-defined path, through kissing gates and along field edges, then drop down to cross a footbridge above rocky Lambsowden Cove. Continue following the rise and fall of the coastal path before joining the road just before Hemmick Beach.

Plan your walk

Bideford
Bude
Launceston
Wadebridge Bodmin
Newquay Liskeard
St Ives Truro St Austell
Falmouth
Penzance
Land's End

DISTANCE: 5 miles (8km)

TIME: 3 hours

START/END: SW975414

TERRAIN: Moderate; one steep climb

MAPS:
OS Explorer 105;
OS Landranger 204

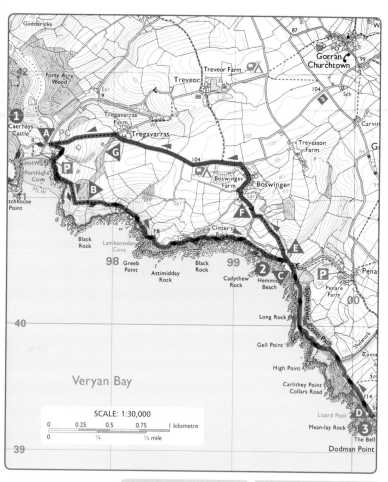

2 The pleasant, sandy beach of Hemmick is generally uncrowded due to limited parking and the lack of immediately available refreshment facilities. There are rock pools at low tide.

C Take the roadside stile on your right before the bend in the road, and follow the path as it rises steadily to Dodman Point.

3 The 370ft (112m) high, heath covered summit of Dodman Point strategically marks the transition between west and east Cornwall. The site was once an Iron Age promontory fort and the open access area on the headland also includes remains of medieval strip fields and Bronze Age barrows. The imposing granite cross was erected

Caerhays & Dodman Point

in 1896 by the Rector of St Michael Caerhays as a guide to seafarers, although there have nevertheless been many shipwrecks off the point.

D ▶ Retrace your steps back to Hemmick Beach, taking care on the descent from Dodman Point.

E ▶ Turn left onto the road. Cross the ford and as the road goes uphill turn right onto the path signposted to Boswinger. Go through the kissing gate and cross two fields.

F ▶ At the lane turn right, and go past the Youth Hostel on your right. At the road junction turn left, past the holiday park on your left, with seasonal shop and café. Continue walking along the lane.

G ▶ After passing the sign entering Tregavarras, at the right hand bend in the road, take the path signposted on your left to Caerhays Beach. Go through the kissing gate and cross the field down to the beach and car park.

Dodman Point

" A short and mostly level walk encircling Pendennis Castle to give fine views from both sides of this strategic headland **"**

This is a gentle stroll round Pendennis Point and back along the road overlooking Falmouth Docks, one of the three largest natural harbours in the world. From the headland there are splendid views across to St Mawes and up the broad inlet of Carrick Roads to St Just-in-Roseland. On the return, below Pendennis Castle, there are equally good views over Falmouth Bay to Penzance Point. You can combine your walk with a visit to the castle, one of the finest fortresses built by Henry VIII. The castle is open April to September but check opening times before visiting.

Falmouth

Pendennis Point

Bideford
Bude
Launceston
Wadebridge Bodmin
Newquay Liskeard
St Ives Truro St Austell
Falmouth
Penzance
Land's End

DISTANCE: 2 miles (3km)

TIME: 1 hour

START/END: SW821322

TERRAIN: Easy

MAPS:
OS Explorer 103;
OS Landranger 204

Route instructions

A Start from the large car park for Pendennis Castle, turning right out of the car park entrance onto Castle Drive. Note that the car park is locked 15 minutes after castle closing time. At the signpost on your left follow the footpath between the road and the shore until it joins the car park at Pendennis Point.

B At the headland the view changes from St Mawes and the mouth of the River Fal to a view across Falmouth Bay to Pennance Point, and beyond to Rosemullion Head.

1 Little Dennis Fort stands at sea level at the tip of the headland. It was probably built in the 1540s to provide auxiliary fire at sea level for

Pendennis Castle, above it. Four guns were placed inside, while others were positioned on the roof. The battlements were designed to lessen the impact of shot by leaning inwards.

C Continue on the road until you reach the 'No Entry' signs (facing away from you) and turn sharply up the drive. This is the entrance point for Pendennis Castle. Go back to the road and resume your former direction, with the sea on your left.

2 Pendennis Castle was begun by King Henry VIII in 1540 and considerably added to by Queen Elizabeth I. Its purpose was to protect the deep,

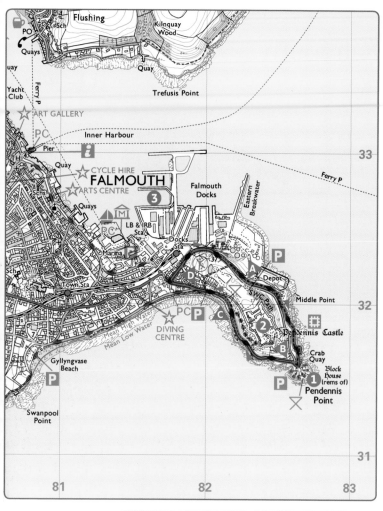

safe anchorage of the Fal estuary from use by enemy fleets. Gales prevented a second Spanish Armada from trying to take this strategic anchorage in 1597, but the castle saw noble action in 1646 when the Royalist Governor, Sir John Arundell, and 900 men, held out for five months against Sir Thomas Fairfax's Roundheads. Over 450 years of history is now on display with exhibitions including a Tudor gun deck, a World War I guardhouse cell and the guns and magazines of Half Moon Battery.

Falmouth

▶ Fork right, downhill away from the sea then turn right up Castle Drive to the car park.

③ Falmouth has been an important port since the days of Sir Walter Raleigh. It provided shelter for ships awaiting favourable winds and was often the first place to replenish the supplies of vessels from across the Atlantic. Fast sailing ships took letters and packets from here to America, Spain and Portugal. The existing docks were built in 1860, when Falmouth was the second busiest port in Britain, after London. The arrival of the railway in 1863 encouraged the growth of tourism.

Falmouth Harbour

> **"** Spectacular coastal walking, with an interesting coastal history, and the distinctive twin-towered lighthouse at Lizard Point as a landmark along much of the way **"**

Walk the coastline of the Lizard peninsula, linking the two main attractions of Kynance Cove and the southernmost tip of Britain at Lizard Point. Then turn inland across farming country, passing through Lizard village to return to Kynance. This area is renowned for its interesting geology, where the largest outcrop of colourful serpentine stone in Britain was formed deep under the Earth's crust before being thrust up about 350 million of years ago. The purple-brown of serpentine can be seen at its best at Kynance, whereas further south it peters out to be replaced by schist in the cliffs and coves along the way. The Lizard is also an area of immense botanical interest, one of the richest in the UK, and in springtime the cliffs are carpeted in the pink, white and blue of wildflowers. The most famous is the pink and purple-flowered heather of Cornish Heath, the county flower of Cornwall that is found growing wild only on the Lizard.

View of the Lizard Lighthouse
from Pen Olver

Lizard Point

Kynance Cove

Route instructions

1 An understandably very popular cove, the beauty of Kynance has been attracting visitors for generations. There are evocative names for features such as Lady's Bathing Pool and the Devil's Letter Box. Geologically the cliffs and stacks of colourful serpentine rock are of considerable interest, but the area is ecologically important too, with several plants found here that are not found anywhere else in Britain.

A Leave the car park to join the cliff path signposted to Lizard Point. Follow the path above Pentreath Beach and continue along the well-defined path towards Polpeor Cove.

2 Polpeor Cove is the site of a disused Victorian lifeboat station. In 1907 this was the scene of the biggest rescue in the RNLI's history when the lifeboat saved 167 lives after the White Star liner *SS Suevic* hit a reef in dense fog. In 1961 the lifeboat station moved to Kilkobban Cove, 1½ miles (2.4km) away.

B Cross the road and continue on the coast path. Turn left at the signpost for the Lizard Lighthouse.

3 The Lizard Lighthouse has guided ships on the English Channel, one of the busiest shipping lanes in the world, along a particularly hazardous coast for over 250 years. The beam can

Plan your walk

DISTANCE: 5 miles (8km)

TIME: 3 hours

START/END: SW689132 Park at Kynance Cove. If visiting Kynance Cove first, follow the signpost to walk down to the cove.

Check tide times for Kynance Cove when planning your walk. The beach is best visited at low tide when stacks and caves are exposed.

TERRAIN: Moderate

MAPS:
OS Explorer 103;
OS Landranger 203

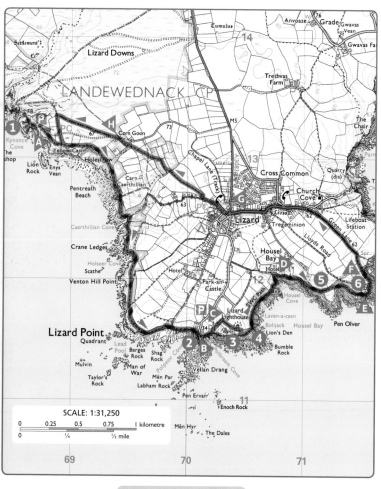

be seen for 26 miles (42km). The renovated engine room now houses the Lighthouse Heritage Centre with exhibitions, interactive displays and tours of the lighthouse tower.

C Take the permissive path that goes around the lighthouse boundary wall, keeping the wall on your right before rejoining the coast path.

4 Lion's Den is an impressive, unfenced 40ft (12m) hole in the cliff, created when a sea cave collapsed one night in 1847.

D Pass above Housel Bay, below the Housel Bay Hotel and continue round the

Lizard Point

path of Pen Olver headland. Look back for stunning views of the lighthouse behind you. Pass the Lizard Wireless Station on your left.

5 Two unremarkable looking black wooden huts on the headland of Pen Olver comprise the oldest surviving purpose-built wireless communications station in the world. Guglielmo Marconi used them for pioneering experiments and in 1901 set a new wireless distance record with a message that had travelled 186 miles from the Isle of Wight. The buildings have been restored by the National Trust and can be visited, although opening times are limited.

E Go round Bass Point Old Signal Station.

6 The unmistakable castellated building of the former Lloyds Signal Station was built in 1872. Over 1000 ships a month used the station in 1878, sailing in close to the point to register their names and collect messages. Although owned by the National Trust it is now a private home.

F Leave the coast path by continuing on the track ahead, through the gate for Churchtown Farm. Pass the farm buildings and turn

left onto the road. Turn left again at the next junction and pass the school on your right.

G In Lizard village go straight across the road, signposted 'coastal footpath', then straight across the next road, signposted 'Kynance Cove'. Bear right onto the signposted track to follow the footpath along the top of a double hedge bank. Bear right again at the footpath junction in the thicket to follow the path slightly uphill. Continue along the well-defined path across fields to reach a stile at the bend of a road.

H Walk straight ahead along the road, signposted to the car park, turning right onto the footpath that runs parallel to the road. As the path joins the track at the edge of the car park either turn left to the car park entrance or right to enter the other end of the car park and the path down to Kynance Cove.

Lloyds Signal Station

This route starts by following one of the streams which feed the head of the Helford Estuary. It then goes across country, with some splendid views, to return to Gweek near a second stream which feeds the Helford. There is plenty of variety, with the welcome presence of trees, but no really steep hills. Allow time to visit the National Seal Sanctuary.

Stream near Tolvan Cross

Gweek

Yachts moored on the Helford River

Route instructions

Plan your walk

DISTANCE: 5 miles (8km)

TIME: 2½ hours

START/END: SW706267

TERRAIN: Easy; but can be muddy in places

MAPS:
OS Explorer 103;
OS Landranger 203

A Gweek is about 3 miles (4.8km) east of Helston, on the B3291. Start from the bus stop at Gweek Quay. Cars can be parked considerately at the roadside nearby. With your back to the bus shelter, go left towards Helston. Walk uphill and across a bridge.

B Turn right up a track signposted public footpath passing old mill buildings on your left. Bear right over a bridge across a stream and follow a track. Pass the last house on your left and bear right over a stile beside a gate. Continue beside a hedge on your right and through two gates. Veer left to go through a gate in the corner ahead. Continue with the hedge on your left to

the corner of the field and veer left to cross a stile. Go through trees emerging into a field.

C Go round the field keeping the hedge on your left to a gate opposite, just below a corner. Go through the gate, along a grassy track. Pass Pollard Mill and follow its drive bearing left along a metalled road to a road. This route continues to the right, uphill along the road, but first divert to your left to see the sluice gate for the mill leat from the bridge. Back on the uphill road, take a concrete track (and cross a cattle grid) on your left to Pollard Farm. Walk with a hedge on your right and a view of a wooded valley on your left.

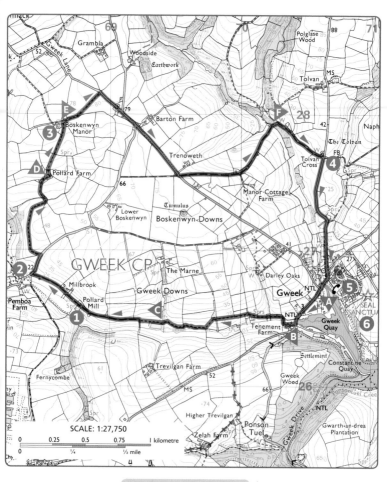

1 Pollard Mill has been partly restored. Its wheel is still visible but there is not enough water supply to keep it running. The leat runs alongside the route to the bridge but is now mainly dry.

2 Here you can see the sluice-gate which enables the stream water to be channelled into the leat.

D Go through the farmyard and fork left to pass the house and barn on your right. Go ahead through a gate and veer slightly right across a field to a stile to the right of electricity supply poles. Cross the stile and continue beside a hedge on your left. At the end of the hedge turn left to reach Boskenwyn Manor.

Gweek

3 When you reach Boskenwyn Manor, look back for a view over to the Goonhilly Satellite Earth Station. Once the largest satellite earth station in the world, satellite operations ceased at Goonhilly in 2008 and many of the dishes have now been dismantled.

E Turn right along a track to a road. Go right. Pass a school on your left and, at a junction, go ahead towards Gweek. Ignore a right fork, then an entrance to Barton Farm on your left. Just past Trenoweth on your left take a hedged track on your left. Descend to a stream.

F Cross the stone slab bridge. Bear right uphill to a road. In the back garden of a house on your left, although out of sight is the Tol-ven stone.Turn right down the road back to Gweek. If visiting the seal sanctuary go ahead up the signposted lane. Retrace your steps to the B3291 in Gweek and turn left to go over the bridge back to the bus shelter.

4 Tol-ven means 'holed stone' in Cornish. Like Men-an-Tol, this stone has a reputation for healing.

5 Gweek used to be an important port. The Phoenician tin traders probably came here, and the Romans built forts nearby. This was for centuries the port of Helston, which was a prosperous borough in the 13th century. Access to its own quays was closed off by the advancing sands of the Loe Bar, making Gweek the natural port. The mining that brought the commerce also deposited waste material in the streams and silted up the River Helford. Cargo ships still made it up here in the 1930s, and barges called here regularly until 1945.

6 When miner Ken Jones took early retirement, he moved with his wife to Cornwall, rescued a seal and went on to create this sanctuary, complete with a special hospital. Now part of the Sea Life chain of aquariums and other sea life themed attractions, the sanctuary has developed greatly since its inception in 1958. It nevertheless still rescues seals and returns as many as possible back to the wild. The hospital has pens and pools where injured seal pups are cared for. The winter is the best time to see them. The sanctuary is open all year but check times and prices before visiting and be aware that there may be locally available vouchers giving discounts on admission.

> **"** This level seafront stroll requires no route finding and although described from Penzance to Marazion, it could easily be done in either direction **"**

The focal point of the walk is St Michael's Mount, rising from the sea in the curving sweep of Mount's Bay. The means of visiting the castle is dependent on tides. At low tide there is a cobbled causeway between Marazion and the isle, so plan your walk accordingly if you want to walk across to the castle. At high tide, in season, there is a crossing by ferry boat, but note that the castle is closed on Saturdays. Once on the isle there is a steep climb to the top, but the main route of this walk is flat with an easy track to follow.

Penzance & St Michael's Mount

Marazion Marsh

Route instructions

A Park in one of the two large Marazion beachfront car parks. Take the bus to Penzance from the bus stop just outside the entrance to the car park nearest St Michael's Mount. There are several bus services, day and evening, between Marazion and Penzance bus station.

1 Penzance is the most westerly major town in Cornwall. There are several museums, including the Trinity House National Lighthouse Centre. Outside the market house is a statue of Sir Humphrey Davy, inventor of the miner's safety lamp, who was born in Penzance in 1778. The mild climate means that many sub-tropical plants thrive in this area, and the sight of palm trees is not unusual.

B Take time to explore the town of Penzance, or to start the walk from the bus station, follow the seafront walkway/cycleway as far as the footbridge near the heliport.

C From here it is possible to either walk along the beach or continue using the track of the N3 National Cycle Network that runs most of the way in between the railway track and the beach.

2 The RSPB Marazion Marsh Reserve, noted for its overwintering wildfowl, is the largest reedbed in

Plan your walk

Bideford
Bude
Launceston
Wadebridge Bodmin
Newquay Liskeard
St Ives Truro St Austell
Falmouth
Penzance
Land's End

DISTANCE: 4 miles (6.5km)

TIME: 2 hours

START/END: SW514308 Marazion car park

TERRAIN: Easy

MAPS:
OS Explorer 102;
OS Landranger 203

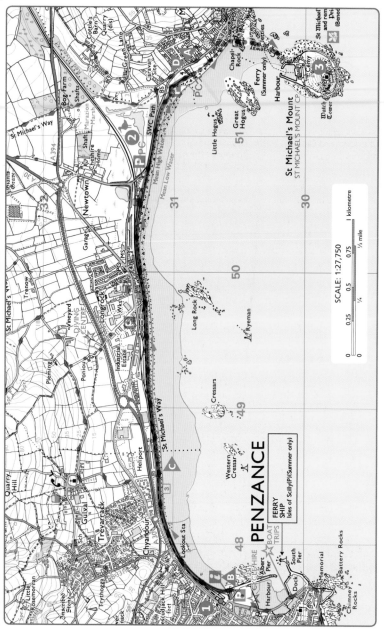

Penzance & St Michael's Mount

Cornwall. Over 250 bird species have been recorded here, including chiffchaff, little egret and Cetti's warbler.

▶ Stop at the car park, or continue ahead to visit St Michael's Mount, either by causeway or ferry boat.

❸ The island is generally identified with the Ictis mentioned by Diodorus Siculus (1st century BC) as the port from which tin was shipped to Brittany. It also has a place in legend as part of the lost kingdom of Lyonesse, a land of fine cities that now lies beneath the sea. The building on the isle has a long history as a priory, fortress and home. It was originally a Benedictine monastery, founded by Edward the Confessor in honour of the saint and as a dependent of the great Abbey of Mont St Michel in Brittany. Suppressed in 1425 it became a fortress and a residence. Since 1659 the Mount has been the seat of the St Aubyn family, who still live there and manage the island. Francis St Aubyn, the 3rd Lord, gave the Mount to the National Trust in 1954 and it is open to visitors daily in the summer, except Saturdays. In winter there is a restricted opening, so check ahead for opening times before visiting.

Mount's Bay

66 Starting from one of Cornwall's most famous ancient monuments follow quiet paths across farmland and along the way pass other examples of prehistoric sites **99**

This route introduces you to the glory of inland Cornwall, especially to the standing stones which characterise West Penwith. Ancient paths using stone stiles to cross old boundary walls lead from the best preserved stone circle in Cornwall. There is a wealth of neighbouring monuments, and it is not far from the start of the walk to Lamorna Cove, from where the coastal path leads to Mousehole.

Merry Maidens

One of the Pipers

Route instructions

1 The Merry Maidens is one of the best preserved stone circles in Britain. Dating from about 2540BC, its stones include only three that had to be re-erected in the 19th century, and they are equally spaced with an entrance gap on the eastern side, where there may have been a processional way. Maiden is a corruption of *meyn* or *men*, meaning stone (and pronounced main in Cornish). Merry is derived from Mary or Mari, the fertile mother worshipped as a goddess in the Middle East in 1000BC. The legend is that some merry maidens were turned to stone for dancing here on a Sabbath. The two Pipers who played the music were also turned into stones.

A Start from the lay by parking at Merry Maidens. Go over the stile to the stone circle. After seeing the standing stones leave this field by a stile in the top right corner. Go ahead to a stile beside a telegraph pole. Emerge at a bend in the road.

B Before continuing the route take a short detour by going straight ahead on the B3315 to see a view of the Pipers standing stones from a farm gate on the left hand side of the road.

2 These two standing stones are known as the Pipers – they who played the tunes for the merry maidens to dance to. They are 15ft (4.5m) high.

Plan your walk

Bideford
Bude
Launceston
Wadebridge Bodmin
Newquay Liskeard
St Ives Truro St Austell
Falmouth
Penzance
Land's End

DISTANCE: 4 miles (6.5km)

TIME: 2 hours

START/END: SW432245

TERRAIN: Easy

MAPS:
OS Explorer 102;
OS Landranger 203

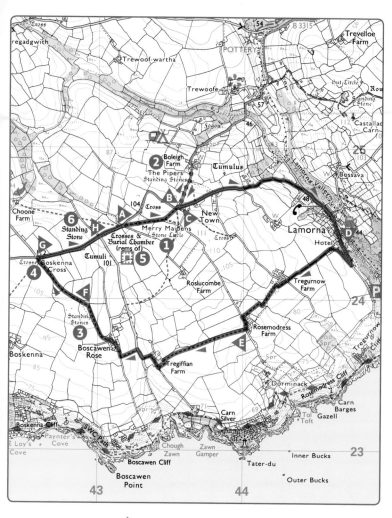

C Return to the junction and turn left up an access lane towards Menwinnion Country House. Continue down an old green lane to the road. Turn right to walk down the road.

D Turn right up the lane signposted to the Cove

Restaurant. Continue to a sharp right turn and go right to pass a house called Tregurno Cliff. Bear left through stone gate posts and along a hedged track. At Tregurnow Farm turn left over a stile. Continue along a field edge past the farm on your right, then bearing left

Merry Maidens

cross a stone stile to join a farm track bearing to your right, with Rosemodress Farm buildings on your left.

▶**E** Turn right and continue alongside a hedge on your right to go over a stile ahead. Follow the field boundary to a step stile in a wall beside a cottage on your right. Cross this and turn right along a lane, passing a farm on your right and around a left-hand bend, then a right-hand bend. Just after this bend, turn left over a stone stile in the hedge. Walk with the hedge on your left to a track and turn right along it to a farm. Walk between buildings with the farmhouse on your right. Go across the farmyard and through a gateway on the right to reach the corner of a field. Ignoring a gate ahead, veer left to the corner of a hedge jutting out into a field on your left. Go ahead with this hedge on your right almost to the far corner, then cross the field to a stile on your left. Go over it and follow a hedge on your left, noticing a standing stone in the field on its other side.

3 The standing stone across the hedge is one of a pair. Rising nearly 9ft (2.7m) out of the ground, it is aligned with the south-west Piper stone and the Merry Maidens stone circle.

▶**F** Cross a stile in the field corner ahead and veer slightly right across the next field and over a stile in the hedge opposite. Cut across a field to join a hedge on your left. Follow the hedge on your left to a stile in the corner and cross it to reach a road. Notice Boskenna Cross on your left.

4 Wayside crosses indicated the routes for travellers in bygone days. Originally this cross would have stood in the middle of the road, aligned with the Merry Maidens and another cross to the west.

▶**G** Turn right on to the road and pass Tregiffian Barrow on your right.

5 Tregiffian Barrow is a Bronze Age tomb, although part of it was destroyed by construction of the road in 1840. When excavated in the 1960s, a cupmarked stone was found and replaced by a concrete replica.

▶**H** Continue along the road to the car park lay by. Before leaving cross the road to a stile opposite the lay by. Go over the stile to see a standing stone in the far corner of the field.

6 This magnificent 10.5ft (3.2m) high standing stone is called Gun Rith, meaning Red Downs.

> **66** Steeped in lore and legend, the granite headland of Land's End has a fascinating atmosphere that has captured people's imaginations for thousands of years **99**

Land's End is a world-famous landmark so choose your time to visit carefully if you want to sense the original isolation of this very popular place. Set off early from Sennen Cove to see Land's End at its quietest, or alternatively you can plan your walk to visit at times when the wealth of attractions are open. From Land's End to Mill Bay you have some of the finest scenery along the South West Coast Path – a good cliff-top track which is well defined in most parts crossing boulder-strewn grass and heather. From April the cliff tops are scattered with wild flowers and in late summer and autumn the way is coloured yellow with gorse and pink with heather. It is understandably a popular section of coast path, but the return route inland from Mill Bay crosses some quiet countryside along easy paths, providing the opportunity to see this headland from another perspective.

Enys Dodnan, Land's End

Sennen Cove & Land's End

Mill Bay

Route instructions

1 Sennen Cove is the most westerly village in England. It once relied heavily on fishing but is now a small resort, although fishing continues on a reduced scale. The lifeboat station was founded in 1853 and is open to visitors in the summer.

A Park at the harbour car park. At the far end of the car park go left of the toilet block, turn left and follow the steps up the hillside to the former coast guard look out.

2 The granite Mayon Lookout was built in 1912. It now provides an information point with fine views north to Cape Cornwall and south to Land's End.

B Continue along the well-defined coast path for 500yds (460m).

3 Wedged in the rocks of Castle Zawn is the rusting hulk of the *RMS Mulheim*, wrecked in 2003 on its way between Ireland and Germany.

4 A short detour from the path leads to the summit of Maen Castle, established in the late Bronze Age and still used in the Iron Age. The restored entrance and remains of stone ramparts are still visible today.

C Continue along the coast path to Dr Syntax's Head then on to the buildings at Land's End.

Plan your walk

DISTANCE: 4½ miles (7.25km)

TIME: 3 hours

START/END: SW355263 Sennen Cove harbour car park

TERRAIN: Moderate

MAPS:
OS Explorer 102;
OS Landranger 203

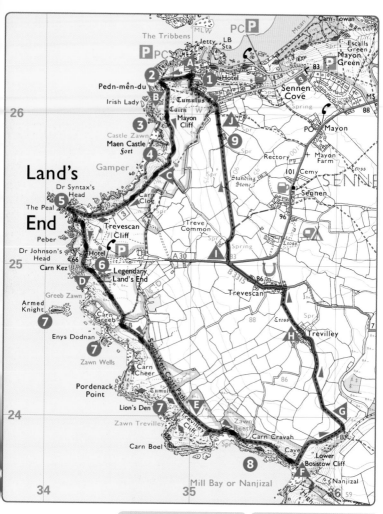

5 Dr Syntax's Head is the most southwesterly point of mainland Britain and so is really the true 'Land's End'. The First and Last House is one of the oldest buildings on the headland and has been serving refreshments since the 19th century.

6 Land's End has long been a draw for tourists but more recently has been developed to emerge as an open-all-year tourist destination. Visitors come to see the famous Land's End signpost and hotel, and can now choose from several pay-as-you-go attractions.

Sennen Cove & Land's End

D Continue on the coast path, with the entrance to Greeb Farm on your left.

7 From the cliff path you can see several interesting features. The rocky isle of Armed Knight is home to razorbills, shags and guillemots, whilst the natural arch of Enys Dodnan has a colony of greater black-backed gulls. Next is Lion's Den, a dramatic fissure in the granite that plunges down to the shore.

E Cross a small stream, round the headland and descend to Mill Bay.

8 Accessible only by foot, the boulder-strewn beach of Mill Bay, is never busy.

F Just before the path drops to cross the stream flowing into Mill Bay, take the path going upwards on the left. Follow the path as it curves its way along the valley side. As the path bends to the left, go over a stile.

G Cross the field to the opening on the far side. Follow the path alongside the hedge on your right. At the field corner go through the opening and cross the field to the hedge in front of you. Follow the path, keeping the hedge on your left. At the corner of the field cross a stone stile and join a track, then an access lane.

H At the lane junction turn right then next left into a farmyard. Go over the stepped stile at the far end of the yard and follow the hedge on your right to another stile. Follow the fence on your left to go through a kissing gate to the B3315 at Trevescan. Turn left and follow the road to the A30 junction.

I Cross the A30 with care and take the track straight ahead to Treeve Moor House. Do not turn bear left into the grounds of the house, but go straight ahead to follow a path bearing right over a stile into a field. The footpath is signposted ahead on a telegraph pole. Go through a kissing gate and cross to the stile next to the gate visible across the field. Cross the next field heading for the white buildings.

9 Trinity House Cottages were built to house the Longships Lighthouse keepers and their families.

J Go over the stile at the end of the cottage wall, turn left and follow the road, going straight ahead onto a track as the road bends right. Follow the track then take the path on your left next to a metal gate, following this to join the path up from Sennen Cove, passing the lookout before descending back down to the car park.

Sennen Cove

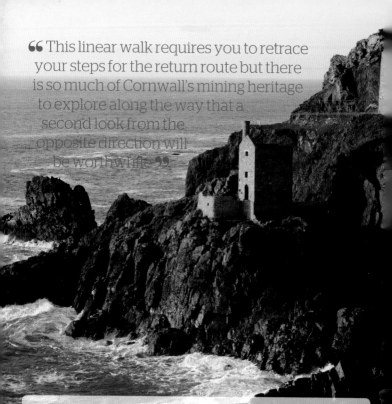

> **❝** This linear walk requires you to retrace your steps for the return route but there is so much of Cornwall's mining heritage to explore along the way that a second look from the opposite direction will be worthwhile **❞**

The entire walk is within the St Just district of the Cornish Mining World Heritage Site, one of the most ancient tin and copper mining areas in Cornwall. The path passes close by to many ruined mine buildings and it is humbling to think of the miles of passages that were once mined under the ground you walk, as well as in tunnels out under the sea.

The route is along high cliffs within an area of mine shafts and old mine buildings, so requires care at all times. Allow plenty of time for this walk, as there is plenty of interest along the way. It is also possible to take a short detour from Levant to visit Geevor, the largest preserved tin mining site in Britain. Check opening hours and prices before visiting.

As well as the historical interest, the cliffs and shore along this route are havens for wildlife. The headlands of Cape Cornwall, Kenidjack and Botallack all provide good lookout points for seals, basking sharks and dolphins, and the cliffs shelter breeding sea birds.

Cape Cornwall & Levant

Botallack Mine

Route instructions

1 With few tourist facilities apart from the car park, toilets and seasonal refreshments van, Cape Cornwall has an evocative setting. There are paths up the headland to the chimney on the summit, which was part of the Cape Cornwall mine that closed in 1870. Despite the name it is not a true cape as the currents of the Atlantic separate to the south, at Gwennap Head, to go north into the Bristol Channel or south along the English Channel.

A From the car park at Cape Cornwall walk back up the road and turn left onto the signposted coast path along a grassy track. Follow the stone coast path marker to turn left along a bracken and gorse lined path. The path curves to follow the valley inland then drops down to cross a stream over a wooden footbridge.

2 The steep sided Kenidjack valley was once an important tin mining area that was mined intensively until the 1870s. The remains of engine houses and arsenic works are still visible. The area is well known for attracting rare birds and is popular with birdwatchers.

B Bear left after the bridge then turn right at the stone marker to walk along the valley, then right at the next stone marker to go uphill. At the next path junction

Plan your walk

Bideford
Bude
Launceston
Wadebridge · Bodmin
Newquay · Liskeard
St Ives · Truro · St Austell
Penzance · Falmouth
Land's End

DISTANCE: 5 miles (8km), includes both outward and return

TIME: 3 hours

START/END: SW353317 Cape Cornwall car park (National Trust)

TERRAIN: Moderate

MAPS: OS Explorer 102; OS Landranger 203

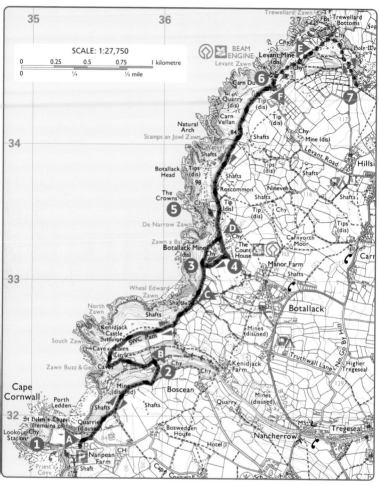

follow the coast path marker to turn left, then next right to go uphill and over a stone stile to pass a ruined building on your left. Continue along a grassy path over another stone stile next to a gate, then left onto a track.

▶ **C** Continue on the path alongside the former

Botallack mine workings, passing the engine houses of Wheal Edward and West Wheal Owles. Take time to explore the side paths around the ruined buildings before continuing.

3 The copper and tin mine of Botallack closed in 1914 after nearly 100 years of activity. Shafts were worked

Cape Cornwall & Levant

far out under the sea. The derelict mine workings that remain are under the protection of the National Trust. Areas to explore include the 1906 tin-dressing floors and the arch–roofed condensing chambers where arsenic was extracted from the tin ore.

4 Botallack Count House, or 'account house' was built in 1862 to provide office space for the mine purser and clerical staff. It now houses information displays about the renovation of the building and the work of the National Trust in the area.

5 From the path is a view of the much-photographed engine houses of the Crowns Mine, perched on the cliff below. The lower engine house, built in 1835, pumped water from the mine and the upper engine house, built in 1862, provided winding power for an undersea shaft.

D Return to the main coast path, which continues north and is well-defined all the way along the cliff top to Levant.

6 The Levant mine produced copper and tin ore until its closure in 1919 after 31 miners were killed in an accident. The mine ran for 1 mile (1.6km) under the sea. Many of the 19th and

early 20th century buildings have been preserved under the care of the National Trust. This includes engine houses, chimney stacks, the tramway and main engine tunnels for transporting miners to deep workings, and powder magazines. In Mitchell's Engine House the beam winding (whim) engine can be seen in operation on publicised 'steaming' days. It is the only Cornish beam engine still working on its original site.

E If desired continue on the coast path for a short detour to visit Geevor. The path passes through the lower end of the site.

7 Geevor was a working tin mine until 1990 and is now one of the largest mining heritage sites in the UK. It is open all year, except Saturdays. There are mine buildings containing machinery and equipment, interactive museum displays, a shop and a café - but the highlight of most peoples visit is usually the tour underground into the late 18th or early 19th century tunnel of Wheal Mexico.

F Retrace your steps, following the coast path all the way back to Cape Cornwall.

West Wheal Owles

> 66 A circular walk exploring the often wild and windswept moorland of inland Penwith passing several notable ancient sites along the way 99

There are prehistoric monuments to entice you on to this walk across open country, and everyone will enjoy the view across Mount's Bay on a fine day. Ding Dong mine is of interest to industrial archaeologists although the engine house ever present on the skyline is all that remains, and the paths across the heather are bracing in all seasons.

Men-an-Tol

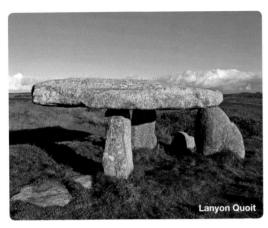

Lanyon Quoit

Route instructions

A Start from the small parking area between Madron and Morvah. Go through the gate and up the signposted track to Men-an-Tol.

B Look for a signposted stile on your right and cross it to follow the path to the Men-an-Tol holed stone. Retrace your steps over the stile to turn right and resume your former direction. After 400yds (365m), notice the Men Scryfa standing stone in the centre of a field on your left.

1 The Men-an-Tol monument is famous for its holed stone, indeed the name means 'Hole Stone' in Cornish. The circular stone, set on its edge and with the hole through it, is on a line between two upright stones, while a fourth stone lies fallen to the north-west of it. This monument may date from the Stone Age or, at least, the Bronze Age, making it up to 6000 years old. The prime function of the stone was magical, rather than astronomical. Holed stones are associated with healing, with the sick person being passed through them.

2 Men Scyrfa means, in Cornish, the stone of writing. It is inscribed with the words 'Rialobrani Cunovali Fili' (the last word is now below ground). This means 'of the Royal Raven, son of the Glorious Prince', dating the inscription to about AD500.

Plan your walk

Bideford
Bude
Launceston
Wadebridge Bodmin
Newquay Liskeard
St Ives Truro St Austell
Falmouth
Penzance
Land's End

DISTANCE: 4½ miles (7.25km)

TIME: 2¼ hours

START/END: SW418344

TERRAIN: Easy

MAPS:
OS Explorer 102;
OS Landranger 203

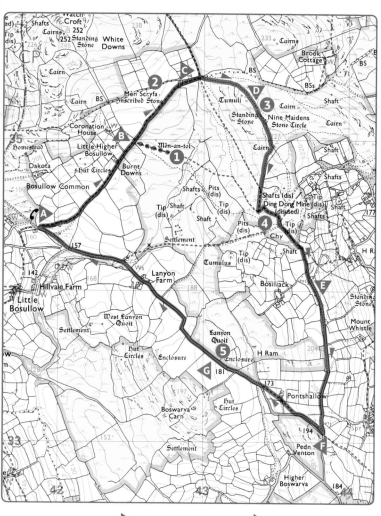

Fork right and pass a derelict cottage on your left. Reach a crosspaths at the Four Parish Stone, at the point where Zennor, Gulval, Madron and Morvah parishes meet. Bear right uphill. Reach the summit and go right, past a round barrow.

Go ahead to the Nine Maidens stone circle. Pass this on your left and soon veer right towards the old Ding Dong mine, the engine house of which is a prominent landmark. Your path lies ahead, passing the engine house on your right, so only divert along the track

Men-an-Tol

bearing right for a closer inspection of the building. Continue down a gravel track. There is a fine view of St Michael's Mount on your left.

3 The Nine Maidens is a stone circle currently consisting of five upright stones, four badly leaning and two fallen. In the mid 18th century, Dr Borlase recorded 13 upright stones and 6 fallen ones. The original total may have been 21 or 22 stones, averaging 4ft (1.2m) in height, with the highest stone being over 6ft (1.8m). The stones were evenly spaced in an accurate circle of 24yds (21.9m).

4 Ding Dong is an ancient tin mine. Its heyday was in the early 19th century. It closed in 1878, due to cheap tin imported from Malaya.

E The gravel track turns into a lane and joins a road about 1 mile (1.6km) south of Ding Dong mine.

F Turn sharply right along the road. Bend left with the road for 100yds (90m), then veer right over a stone stile and cross a field to another stone stile. Go ahead over a farm drive and cross a wire fence (access is permitted). Descend to a stile in the corner ahead. Go over it to return to the road, where you bear right. Pass Lanyon Quoit on your right.

5 Lanyon Quoit is a classic example of this type of monument. It is also a highly-restored specimen which differs significantly from the known original. When Dr Borlase came here in the mid 18th century, it consisted of a capstone 19ft (5.8m) long supported by four stones tall enough to allow a man on horseback to pass under it. This fell during a violent storm in 1815, breaking one of its stone supports. Local people subscribed to have the capstone re-erected in 1824.

G Continue past Lanyon Farm and tearoom to the parking area where you started.

Ding Dong tin mine

❝ Enjoy a gentle stroll along the coast to St Ives, then return on a scenic train ride around Carbis Bay **❞**

This is a lovely short walk linking the beautiful sandy beaches of St Ives. The way is mostly level, apart from an optional deviation round the headland at St Ives, and there are splendid views from several points along the coast. In summer the town of St Ives can get crowded and parking can be difficult. This walk avoids the need for town centre parking and instead you can park at the station to combine an easy walk with a short train trip and the opportunity to explore an historic and picturesque town the best way there is - on foot.

St Ives

St Ives from the coast path

Route instructions

A Park at Carbis Bay rail station car park. Turn left out of the car park and go down the road to Carbis Bay beach. Take the path between the Sands Café and the Carbis Bay Hotel and follow it around the hotel to cross the footbridge over the railway.

B Continue along the path, going straight on when it joins a narrow lane. On your left you pass The Baulking House.

1 The white-painted Baulking House is a former fisherman's lookout from where the 'huer' watched for shoals of pilchards in the bay so he could alert townsfolk below to launch their fishing boats.

C As the lane bends to the left take a short detour to the right, down a road marked 'Private Road Pedestrians Only' for a panoramic view of Porthminster Beach and St Ives. Retrace your steps to continue downhill on the signposted path. Cross the railway bridge and at the path junction take the way ahead as it drops down to Porthminster Beach.

D For an immediate return journey by train, climb the steps on your left to the railway station. Alternatively continue along the beachfront to the centre of St Ives.

2 St Ives is one of the best-known Cornish resorts. The town is named after the

Plan your walk

DISTANCE: 3 miles (4.75km)

TIME: 2 hours

START/END: SW528387 Carbis Bay rail station car park. The single-track St Ives Bay Line runs regularly throughout the day and evening, hugging the coast between St Erth and St Ives. Plan ahead with a timetable available online or locally, and check return train times at the station when you park.

TERRAIN: Easy

MAPS:
OS Explorer 102;
OS Landranger 203

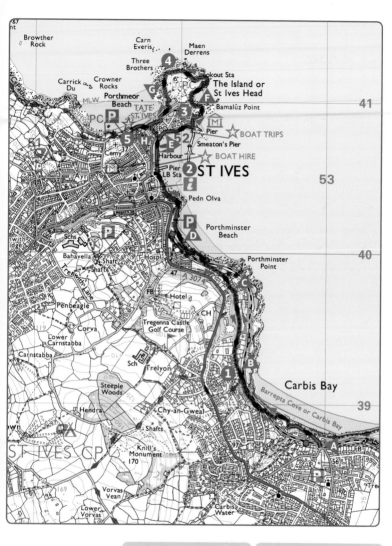

Irish St Ia who landed here in AD460 on a Christian mission and St Ives grew up around the small 6th century chapel of St Ia. The livelihood of the town depended on pilchard fishing until the 1890s when the coming of the railway made it a popular holiday and residential town. John Smeaton, the famous builder of the third Eddystone Lighthouse, constructed the harbour in 1770 and St Leonards

St Ives

Chapel on the pier is the traditional chapel for St Ives fishermen. It is easy to see why this picturesque and colourful port has attracted artists for generations, making it famous as an artistic centre. There is a wealth of art studios and small galleries to visit, as well as the internationally acclaimed Tate.

E Follow the road round the harbour, turning left at Smeaton's Pier. Keep to the sea wall, passing the museum on your left.

3 The traditional style St Ives Museum is run by enthusiastic volunteers and is a treasure trove collection of all kinds of artefacts related to local history, farming, fishing, lifeboats, shipwrecks and mining. The site of the museum has a long history including use as a chapel, pilchard-curing cellar and as accommodation for shipwrecked mariners.

F Continue following the sea wall round the small beach of Porthgwidden, then take the path up from the car park to climb the headland of the Island.

4 At the top of the Island there are panoramic views along the coast. The National Coastwatch Institution runs the watch station voluntarily. The adjacent remains of battery fortifications were built in 1860 to guard against a possible French invasion by Napoleon. The original chapel of St Nicholas was destroyed and the existing building dates from 1911.

G Take the path back down the headland and turn right to follow the road, or alternatively walk along the beach, to the Tate St Ives gallery facing onto Porthmeor Beach.

5 Tate St Ives is a landmark white building, opened in 1993. Housing the finest modern and contemporary paintings, sculptures and ceramics, it also hosts family activities and interactive talks.

H Follow the narrow streets back to the harbour, taking time to wander the colourful streets of the town before retracing your steps along the harbour and back to the railway station.

Chapel of St Nicholas, St Ives Head

> **“** Some excellent cliff-top walking, noted for its fine views and wildlife, with the added interest of the remains of mine workings along the way **”**

This is a one-way route so you will need to plan your walk carefully as it is dependant on bus times. The described route suggests parking at Porthtowan and catching a bus to St Agnes to walk the coastal path back to Porthtowan. Check bus timetables for bus service 315 (Redruth – St Agnes) before starting your walk, noting that the service does not run in the evenings or Sundays.

The way follows the well-signposted coast path, so is not difficult to follow, but does split at several places to explore points of interest, generally rejoining a little further along the route. Although the landscape is rugged it is not difficult walking, and there are several benches along the route to take a rest. The path passes National Trust owned Wheal Coates, one of the best known of Cornwall's cliff-top mine buildings.

Porthtowan beach

St Agnes to Porthtowan

Wheal Coates

Route instructions

1 The small town of St Agnes was a thriving centre during the mining boom. Between 1710 and 1730 and between 1798 and 1916 there was a harbour at Trevaunance Cove, both attempts ultimately washed away by Atlantic storms. The last one was built in response to the copper mining boom, but it also enabled the development of the pilchard industry in the town.

A Get off the bus at the terminus near the St Agnes Hotel. Walk up Trevaunance Road then right onto Rocky Lane. Turn left at the signpost for the coast path to Chapel Porth. Bear right at the second coast path signpost and walk along the metalled road between houses above

Trevaunance Cove. Climb steep steps to the top of the headland. Follow the path past disused quarries on your left and continue past Newdowns Head towards St Agnes Head.

2 Look out for the conical caps over the disused mine shafts of the Polberro complex of tin and copper mine workings which provided employment for 450 people in 1838 and was in full production in the mid 18th century.

B Take the right fork just before the lookout station and walk past the car park at St Agnes Head.

3 St Agnes Head has around 900 pairs of kittiwakes

Plan your walk

Bideford
Bude
Launceston
Wadebridge Bodmin
Newquay Liskeard
St Ives Truro St Austell
Falmouth
Penzance
Land's End

DISTANCE: 5 miles (8km)

TIME: 2½ hours

START/END: SW693480 Park at Porthtowan car park and catch a bus to St Agnes from the stop next to the telephone box on Beach Road.

TERRAIN: Moderate

MAPS:
OS Explorer 104;
OS Landranger 203

nesting on the cliffs below. Also to be seen are herring gull, guillemot and fulmar as well as grey seals and an occasional basking shark. On your left was Cameron Camp, which was used as a practice camp during World War II by the Royal Artillery, and later as a camp for American army units prior to relocating to France. There is a plaque to the memory of Andrew Dunklin who

St Agnes to Porthtowan

plunged to his death over the cliffs here in 1978 while giving his girlfriend a driving lesson. She managed to scramble clear just before the car fell to the sea.

C Notice more capped mine shafts and shortly see the old mine buildings of Wheal Coates. Either stay on the coast path to pass the restored engine house or head towards the National Trust information board and ruined buildings further up the hill.

4 Perched on the cliffs, Wheal Coates ('wheal' being the Cornish for mine) is one of the most dramatically sited of Cornwall's old engine houses. It dates from the 1870s with mine workings just below the low water mark. Despite an attempt to restart viable production in 1911, it was not successful. The ruins comprise the pumping and winding houses dating from 1872, the engine house, which was built in 1880, and the calciner from the second phase of production in 1913.

D Take the right fork just after Wheal Coates, following the acorn signs. Just before descending to Chapel Porth, there is a fine viewpoint overlooking the beach. Descend the steep path to the car park.

5 At the foot of the steep valley is the sandy bay of Chapel Porth. There are rock pools and caves to explore at low tide, and a popular beach café.

E At the end of the car park, next to the café, go over the wooden bridge and follow the coast path sign to Porthtowan. The path heads inland then bends sharply to the right to climb uphill. Once over the headland pass spoil heaps and take the short detour on your left to see the ruin of Wheal Charlotte.

6 Wheal Charlotte opened in around 1820 or 1830 to mine copper, but is believed to have ceased production in the mid 1800s. The remaining wall of the engine house that you can see is the 'bob wall', where the beam of the engine pivoted.

F Return to the main path and keep to the cliff top as the coastal path crosses the headland and descends to the beach and car parks at Porthtowan.

7 Porthtowan is a developing resort with a sandy beach popular with surfers. 'Porth' means landing place and 'towan' means sand dunes. In 1998 a 700lb leatherback turtle was washed up on the shore and is now on display in St Agnes Museum.

> 66 This is fine cliff-top walking along a dramatic length of coastline, with the highlight of Bedruthan Steps halfway along the route 99

To complete this walk without retracing your steps back to the start, park at Mawgan Porth and take a bus to Porthcothan so that you can walk the coast path back to your car. Western Greyhound service 556 (Newquay – Padstow) runs hourly throughout the day between Mawgan Porth and Porthcothan but check times online or with a locally available timetable when planning your walk.

The coastal path along this section is clear and the path straightforward, but the cliff-top can be exposed, with sheer drops to the sea below, so be careful in windy weather.

Porthcothan to Mawgan Porth

Porthcothan Beach

Route instructions

A Park at the beach car park in the small resort of Mawgan Porth. Turn right out of the car park onto the road, then turn right at the next road. The bus stop has no sign but is opposite the putting green, between the village hall and the road junction on the opposite side of the road from the bus stop for Newquay.

B Get off the bus at Porthcothan. From the bus stop, next to the telephone box, take the sandy path to the beach. Branch left in the dunes to pick up the coast path. The path continues along and above the south shore of the beach, climbing gradually before descending to Porth Mear.

1 The long, narrow bay of Porthcothan is sheltered by a small dune system. There is a large expanse of sand at low tide, making it a popular family beach.

2 At Porth Mear there is a good example of a 'sanding lane', evidence of the times when farmers collected lime-rich sand from the beach to transport back to spread on acidic fields.

C At Porth Mear cross the stream over a footbridge and continue to Park Head.

3 The small mounds on this grassy headland are remnants of an Iron Age cliff-top castle, one of many along the headlands of north Cornwall.

Plan your walk

DISTANCE: 4½ miles (7.25km)

TIME: 2½ hours

START/END: SW850672 Mawgan Porth car park

TERRAIN: Moderate

MAPS: OS Explorer 106; OS Landranger 200

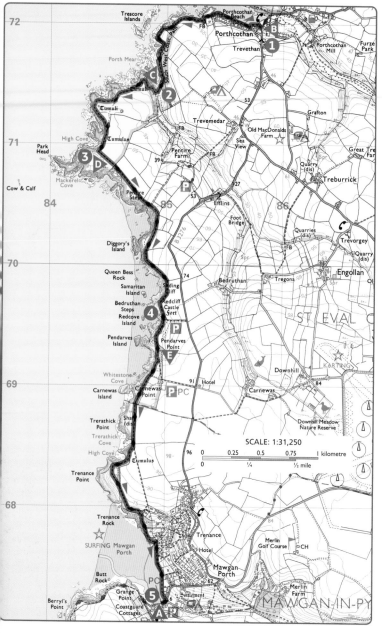

Porthcothan to Mawgan Porth

▶ After descending Park Head you pass Pentire Steps where a zig-zag path used to lead down to the beach until it was destroyed by landslides. Approaching Bedruthan are the remnants of Redcliffe Castle, another Iron Age promontory fort. A short distance further along the coastal path and you will come to Bedruthan Steps.

4 Bedruthan Steps are rock islands of volcanic origin left isolated through erosion. The legend is that the stacks are the stepping stones of the giant Bedruthan, although this may well be a 19th century invention. The site became popular in Victorian times when visitors came in their carriages, and it is still one of the most visited sites in the area. The access steps down to the beach have suffered from erosion over the years but are now secure using netting to hold back rockfall. However, they are closed through the winter and at other times of risk. At the National Trust Carnewas site on the cliff top there is a car park, shop, toilets and refreshments in season.

This part of the coast was particularly hazardous for shipping before the Trevose Lighthouse was built in 1847. The brig *Samaritan*, with a cargo of cotton and silks was wrecked off the Steps in 1846 with only two survivors. For months afterwards, the locals were decked out in finery looted from the wreck. They heartlessly named it *The Good Samaritan* and one of the Steps is known as Samaritan Island.

▶ Continuing from Bedruthan, the path runs through gorse and heather on the cliff-top to return down to the beach at Mawgan Porth.

5 The sheltered resort of Mawgan Porth has a good sandy beach and has become a popular centre for surfing. As with Porthcothan the extent of sand at low tide and the level access to the beach mean that this is also a favourite place for families in summer. Cafés and other facilities are available.

Bedruthan Steps

> 66 This section of cliff path provides fine walking, with the highlight being the spectacular twin headlands of The Rumps' 99

This is a walk with varied geological interest as the path follows the coastline of this unusually shaped headland. Along the way are exposed pillow lavas serving as a reminder of a volcanic past when these rocks were created by underwater vents 350 million years ago. All the land covered by this walk is owned and managed by the National Trust, who have encouraged more traditional and less intensive farming methods to increase biodiversity, especially in arable areas on the headland.

View across Padstow Bay

The Rumps & Pentire Point

The Rumps

Plan your walk

Bideford
Bude
Launceston
Wadebridge Bodmin
Newquay Liskeard
St Ives Truro St Austell
Falmouth
Penzance
Land's End

DISTANCE: 5 miles (8km)

TIME: 2½ hours

START/END: SW941800 Old Lead Mines car park (National Trust) at Pentireglaze

TERRAIN: Moderate

MAPS:
OS Explorer 106;
OS Landranger 200

Route instructions

1 Pentireglaze is the site of old mine workings, the largest and oldest in the area. Rich silver-lead ore was mined here from the 15th or 16th century to 1857.

A Park in the National Trust car park at Pentireglaze. Follow the path next to the notice board to go out of the car park and across a field. Turn left when you join the coast path.

B Continue on the path until a detour to the right takes you over the narrow neck of land where the The Rumps joins the main headland. Follow the paths up and around the promontory.

2 The outline of the impressive Rumps cliff

castle, a fortified settlement of the Iron Age or even earlier, can be seen to advantage from the path. A triple rampart across the neck of the headland defended access; the position of the entrances can also be made out. Excavations have produced pottery from the 1st century BC to the 1st century AD and traces of round houses have been found between the ramparts. The offshore rock to the northeast of the headland is The Mouls, home to breeding puffins, kittiwakes and gannets in summer.

C Return to the main coast path and continue following it with the sea on your right, through two gates and on towards Pentire Point.

walk 20 The Rumps & Pentire Point 93

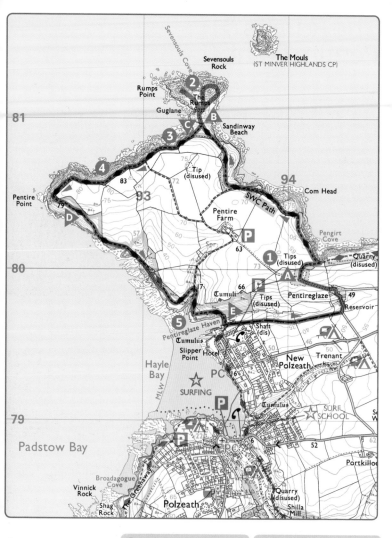

3 A plaque marks the area where the poet Laurence Binyon composed his most famous work, *'For the Fallen'* in 1914. The fourth verse, starting *'They shall grow not old, as we that are left grow old'* is inscribed on many war memorials and recited in Remembrance Services around the world every year.

4 The rock formation changes along this section of path. The sedimentary

The Rumps & Pentire Point

slates and shales give way to once-molten igneous rocks. The rocks at Pentire Point itself are magnificent 'pillow' lavas representing the fossilised outpourings of a once massive submarine volcano.

D You now turn southeast as the coast path descends. Cross a stream at a rocky inlet and continue round the bend to the bay of Pentireglaze Haven.

5 Pentireglaze Haven. This small sandy beach provides more geological interest, with the surrounding slate cliffs revealing interesting colour bandings and faults.

E At Pentireglaze Haven cross the wooden footbridge and turn left to go inland, following the track signposted to Pentireglaze. As the track bends right, continue ahead, through a gate and across two fields keeping the field boundary on your right. Go through a gate to join an enclosed path with a hedge to the left and fence to the right. Emerging onto a road turn left and follow the road, bearing left at the fork to return to the car park.

Route marker

Pentire Point

Photo credits

**All photographs © HarperCollins Publishers Ltd,
photographer Jenny Slater, with the exception of:**